# *An Eagles Wing.*

## *A Scots-Irish Saga.*

William Skidmore Ewing

## CONTENTS.

| | |
|---|---|
| Chapter 1.1 | 1 |
| A Car Journey.1 | 1 |
| Chapter 2.1 | 17 |
| Our Beautiful Homeland.1 | 17 |
| Chapter 3.1 | 23 |
| A Kinsman in Dunstaffanage. 1 | 23 |
| Chapter 4.1 | 29 |
| Callander to Stirling.1 | 29 |
| Chapter 5.1 | 33 |
| Cousins. 1 | 33 |
| Chapter 6.1 | 36 |
| The Battle of Langside.1 | 36 |
| Chapter 7. 1 | 42 |
| Avoiding Death.1 | 42 |
| Chapter 8.1 | 48 |
| Nostalgia Gartcosh.1 | 48 |
| Chapter 9.1 | 56 |
| The Old Man.1 | 56 |
| Chapter 10.1 | 65 |
| His Name Was George. 1 | 65 |
| Chapter 11. 1 | 73 |
| Family Tradition.1 | 73 |
| Chapter 12. 1 | 77 |
| A Brick Wall.1 | 77 |
| Chapter 13.1 | 89 |
| An Irish Orphan.1 | 89 |
| 14. Chapter. 1 | 96 |
| Eagle Wing. 1 | 96 |
| Chapter 15. 1 | 100 |
| Not an Act of God.1 | 100 |
| Chapter 16.1 | 103 |
| America.1 | 103 |
| Chapter 17. 1 | 107 |
| Aristocracy.1 | 107 |
| Chapter 18. 1 | 110 |
| The Main Man.1 | 110 |

Chapter 19. 1 .................................................................114
Scots-Irish. 1 ...............................................................114
Chapter 20. 1 .................................................................118
Stirling Castle.1 ..........................................................118
Chapter 21. 1 .................................................................121
A Reverend in the Family.1 .......................................121
Chapter 22. 1 .................................................................124
Flag-Bearer.1 ..............................................................124
Chapter 23. 1 .................................................................127
A Gathering. 1 ............................................................127
Chapter 24. 1 .................................................................132
Anti-Climax. 1 ...........................................................132
Chapter 25. 1 .................................................................136
Emigration.1 ...............................................................136
Chapter 26. 1 .................................................................142
Robert Ewing. 1 .........................................................142
Chapter 27. 1 .................................................................151
American Civil War.1 ................................................151
Chapter 28. 1 .................................................................155
Still in America. 1 ......................................................155
Chapter 29. 1 .................................................................160
Salamanca. 1 ..............................................................160
Chapter 30. 1 .................................................................188
Clan Ewing. 1 .............................................................188
Epilogue.1 ...................................................................194

# Introduction

This is it? A pull no punches, awesome, honest and down to earth run of the mill story that will hit the headlines.

When it is read there will be a "Trouble at Mill" reaction and the few friends I have I will probably lose. Be warned my theories and conclusions are both controversial; so, let me declare beforehand;

-With hand on my heart I in no way wish to hurt anyone's feelings; but if I do? it is unintentional and I hereby categorically apologize-.

Now I can say what I like? well within reason.

I will start honourably and avoid diving in at the deep end by introducing you to a softening up process. Just my way of creating a lull before the storm, as they say.

One of my favourite singers; Louis Armstrong, I could listen to him all day, he sings the way I try to write. Natural and unforced. This wonderful song of his would have been so appropriate as a beginning to my story, unfortunately I can only state the lyrics; I am sure you will know it so give it a go and sing it along with me.

I quote.

> I see trees of green, red roses too.
> I see them bloom for me and for you.
> And I think to myself
> What a wonderful world.
> I see skies of blue and clouds of white.
> The bright blessed day, the dark sacred night.
> And I think to myself. -What a wonderful world-

> The colours of the rainbow, so pretty in the sky.
> Are also on the faces of people going by.
> I see friends shaking hands saying How-do-you-do?
> They're really saying I love you.
> I hear babies cry; I watch them grow.
> They'll learn much more than I'll ever know.
> And I think to myself -What a Wonderful World-.

The words are so pertinent and he sings from his heart and soul. I play it and join in over and over while driving alone.

Yes; what a wonderful world we are graced with and like me I hope you are living life happily with a loving family. Louis sings about the trees, roses and a beautiful rainbow. Very appropriate; so much my way of thinking. There is nothing more delightful on a sunny day than to sit in the flower garden and enjoy their beauty and fragrance. His mention of babies is again so relevant, watching them grow is the calling of all parents and only for the love and affection of them and our ancestors we would not have had the privilege of life on this amazing and wonderful world.

Yes; the words from that wonderful song pull the heart strings. They also have me thinking of how different life would have been if in my younger days I had shown a bit more appreciation to my parents for their dedication in ensuring that I became what I am today. Samuel and Florence; I owe them so much.

I know it is a bit hypocritical of me to be after the event sorry for not giving them more affection. I could not have wished for better parents. They lived through difficult times, war, rationing, bombs, industrial strikes, tuberculosis and polio to name but a few. I, like everyone else should be very grateful to the wonderful people who brought us into this wonderful world with its beautiful rainbows.

As one gets older one gets more emotional. I find a tear in the eye comes pretty easily and more-so when I'm reminiscing about my ancestors. I hope my story will give you the reader similar feelings and of course the urge to write.

Of course, our world has attributes other than its beautiful nature and they are believed by many to be very detrimental rather than wonderful, but for a by his sell-buy-date pensioner like me, they make life much more pleasant and easier?

Yes, the advances in technology have been extraordinarily wonderful and amazing and it is still expanding at an unbelievable rate. Just think about it; they put a man on the moon during my generation.

In the forefront of all these discoveries and inventions was of course the means of sending information through great distances by radio waves by bouncing them off satellites. A fantastic finding which also brought about the introduction of Web-sites, Apps and many other network systems.

What am I getting at you might ask?

Well it's simply this and I cannot emphasise it enough; our generation is the first to have the opportunity to make use of all these wonderful innovations. The means are there to discover the past, put it into writing and have it published cheaply and easily.

I believe someone in every family should take advantage of the world of computers, to discover and record as much as they can about their present-day family and their ancestors. I don't mean that bore you to tears stuff that's normally written. My idea is for the writings to be creative, interesting; exciting, funny and don't forget, a little bit of hearsay-gossip for the faultfinders and critics.

If you know nothing about recent ancestors, then like me before my research, you should feel ashamed. Get with it, take advantage of Word, Kindle-Self-Publishing and all the other fantastic programmes.

Now isn't that a stupid way to start a book? discrediting the reader. I'm sorry it's just the way Ah tell em and it's just me attempting to shame you into having a go. Honestly the personal gratification and pleasure achieved in carrying out the research is worth it, and once one catches the bug there is no cure, the urge to find out more is always with you.

Wouldn't you have loved to have known your ancestors, stupid question of course, but believe me, Genealogy is the next best thing, you will become engrossed and strive to find out more. How often have you been sitting indulging in a pint when the conversation starts with someone remembering a long-lost friend and commences "Ah mind the time" the reminiscing then goes on until closing time.

Its human nature to be inquisitive about the past especially where family is concerned. Here you have the opportunity to give it a go, I'll bet your family and descendants will be appreciative, might even buy you a pint.

As I said in my description my objective is to have my book sufficiently interesting such that not only my family but everyone will enjoy. You could also easily achieve this and my book will help enormously.

I'm sure you have read Alex Haley's book Roots; his work was a great inspiration to me. It is a terrific example of what a family history record should look like, not just a catalogue of birth and death certificates, but a compilation including adventure and history. To be honest, I am probably being stupid to admit it but you would probably be better using Roots as reference rather than mine. Anyway, I have literally taken a leaf from him and I will be copying his style and my book is less expensive, so you will not go wrong by reading both of them.

Where was I? Oh yes, I was being a bit conceited and why not?

I remember while in English class I received six of the best (strap) for falling asleep. The subject bored me to tears, nouns, adverbs and adjectives didn't see the need. The point being I am no whiz-kid with credentials for writing, my education was such that I became a Mining Mechanical Engineer where the main challenge was how to use a hammer and chisel.

Sorry, something I cannot control; I tend to sway away from the main objective occasionally. This is supposed to be an introduction, an explanation into what my book is all about.

Ok-Doc its Genealogy, no not Gynaecology, let's be serious, simple error, two very similar sounding words with completely opposite meanings, one deals with past life, the other future.

Genealogy, isn't that a terrific word it just seems to roll off the tongue it's so descriptive and pertinent. A Gene is a unit of heredity which is passed from a parent to an offspring and DNA is more or less a way of measuring its strength and origin. I know it's hard for some of us to believe, but I'm sorry to say, eventually we will all die. Do we come back? that is debateable? what is positive is that we do leave a little of ourselves in the form of DNA. Yes, and even our ancestors from way back have passed on to us that little bit of themselves.

If you are really serious about family history getting into a DNA group in Ancestor.Co is advised but not totally necessary (it is quite expensive).

I'm maybe rabbiting on a bit again but what it's all about is family.

What do you think so far? are you convinced? No, OK, let me put it this way. Who looked after you throughout your childhood? who looked after your father throughout his? etc; etc; I could go on and on, we were all loved by our parents, we were family and brotherly love was inborn, I have grandchildren and I love them to bits just as I believe my far off ancestors due to that little bit of passed down DNA would also have loved them. So, let's show respect to our family and get writing.

At one time only a professional could have made up a family tree and it would have cost an arm and leg. Computers and websites changed this, now its oh so easy to put it together. Another great site for family history by the way, Genes Reunited.

Are you considering it? Come on; instead of sitting in gloating about the terrible weather join Ancestry or Scotland's People, put in your personal details and low and behold you are on the road

What has my research done for me? Well I have made friends with many distant cousins mainly from America and even had the privilege of meeting a few of them here in Scotland. Their distant ancestors who were also mine emigrated to America at least 200yrs ago. In fact, some were among the first to cross the pond almost 400yrs ago and they helped to establish colonies in Virginia and other parts of America.

I will be giving a more substantial account of my meetings throughout the book.

Also writing this book has given me a terrific sense of satisfaction, I have achieved something I would not have believed possible only a few years ago. Anyway, I do not want to appear conceited I know my standing, I'm an ex-coalminer and proud of it.

What else has my research done for me?

Other than self-satisfaction it has highlighted my awareness that we should be proud of our heritage and we should all respect our ancestors even if they were not as honest as we would have liked.

To complete my introduction, I will give you a legend I discovered which caused a lot of criticism and debate with members of the "Ewing Family Association of America" they decided it was a hoax. I don't care, our name originated somewhere and I prefer it to some of the other suggestions I've heard and for the non-Ewing's it is a fine example of the wonderful items that can be found on the web.

I quote;

A group of Celts made their home along the eastern shores of Loch Lomond, Scotland. They were peaceful shepherds, tending sheep in the rugged land that had been their proud home. The quiet of the village was shattered by the screech of a huge eagle that swooped from the sky to steal their sheep.

When the eagle boldly took an infant child, the men of this group became the hunters and sought their prey with great determination. The huge bird's nest was located under the ledge of a cliff. This difficult position did not deter the men from their task, and one of the shepherds was lowered by rope over the edge of the cliff. His intention was to kill the great eagle that had plagued their peaceful settlement. Once the mission was complete, he tried to bring the body of the eagle up with him but could not remove the huge bird. Instead, he cut a wing from the eagle and returned with the proof of his deed. Following this sequence of events, the proud group called the rescued baby boy Eagle Wing. The name was shortened throughout the years to E-Wing, and finally settled on the simple spelling of Ewing.

Yes, this is supposedly a Legend, maybe even a bit of nonsense, aren't they all. I don't care. I love it, let the critics have their say and have them prove it wrong.

Like the American Indians, our Ancestors gave names to individuals corresponding to some event. Why not the Picts or whatever? Until someone comes up with proof that this name heritage is incorrect, it will be my reply to how our name came about. If you are an Ewing like me and want to believe it; get yourself a lucky charm of an eagle. I'm a bit of a romantic, I wear one on my bracelet.

Are you still singing? Join with me;

> The colours of the rainbow so pretty in the sky are also on the faces of people going by. I see friends shaking hands saying how-do-you-do, they're really saying I love you and I think to myself what a wonderful world.

I am dedicating my work not only to my parents but to my ancestors. With a bit of luck this book will be their memorial which will be (I hope) appreciated by future generations.

I hope after you read my story, we will still be friends and you will offer to shake my hand.

# Chapter 1.

# A Car Journey.

Isn't the human being a wonderful and awesome piece of wonderment, as an engineer I can appreciate how difficult it would be to design and produce such a specimen. I am not a religious person but surely there must have been something which brought about our creation. The subject I am sure would cause a bit of debate amongst our top intellectuals and not that long ago to even have suggested anything other than the religious belief would have ended up with being ceremoniously burned at the stake. In fact, I wonder, what was this old defenceless lady's offence?

The last witch to be put to death in Scotland, Elspeth McEwan. She was tortured until she confessed; then strangled and burned in Kirkcudbright in 1698. Was she claiming to foresee the future? Was she putting spells on others? Or did someone simply have a grudge?

Do you believe in the supernatural? Is it possible Elspeth haunts the people responsible for her execution? I hope so. Do you believe it possible to sit around a table holding hands and have a conversation with Elspeth or a distant ancestor? Maybe not, but and there are many buts, a lot of people believe and there are a lot of instances where people state they have had unexplainable occurrences with the afterlife.

Wouldn't it be nice to turn a cheeky little brat into a mouse? I'd take the chance of being burned at the stake if I could achieve that.

There is on record a so-called witch from Harrogate who claimed she could converse with the deceased and foresee future events. Mother Shipton was born 1488. She amazingly predicted cars, planes and computers centuries ahead of her time as well as major historic events like the Great Fire of London.

Just a few feet from the cave where she lived is a Petrifying Well which has the power to turn everyday objects to stone. It's strange but true, there is an explanation of course. Water coming through the strata has a limestone content, quite a gimmick though for mother Shipton.

What am I getting at? Well maybe the witches were frauds, were they psychic, I don't think so. What they were doing was playing on people's inquisitive need for knowledge. Its human nature, history, legends you name it. We all strive for it.

I maybe cannot foretell the future, what I do have is the ability to discover the past and I am going to take advantage of it. I have the means to go back in time and my little write up is going to give you the reader a little bit of, not to be statistical or boring but interesting, historical, amusing and of course edge of the seat exciting stuff.

Life is such a wonderful gift; I have been very fortunate in reaching my seventy-eighth year and for an ex-coalminer that's quite an achievement. Having researched into my family I have discovered that I have lived longer than any of my direct line forefathers. Of course, they didn't have my advantage, that of heart medication and a pacemaker implant.

The number of generations our families have covered are uncountable, back to when our ancestors were hitting their female mate with a club and dragging them back to their cave and we have every one of them to thank for our own existence.

It is said we are descendants of apes, if that is the case? how many thousands if not millions of years has it taken for us to have developed into present day humans. Scientists are still working on it, in fact they just recently discovered that we have been walking upright for thousands if not millions of years longer than was previously thought.

I can't take you back that far, although my DNA analysis from Ancestry states I originate from the middle east? are there any monkeys out there?

Ok, Let's get down to it, let's start by giving you your monies worth.

On my seventy seventh birthday Margaret my wife and I decided to have a few days away, as it was my big day I decided for a bit of nostalgia, onto the banks of Loch Fyne where it is said my ancestors, maybe even the ape like ones originated.

By the way I am going along with the theory that the Ewing's and McEwan's were family, having found no evidence to substantiate this, I personally doubt it.

On this occasion I will go along with the historians and pay Loch Fyne a visit. Here's a piece of statistical information which goes way back and more or less verifies the existence of a stronghold on the site we are intending visiting.

I quote from an old account.

> The headland on which McEwan's Castle sat rises steeply from the foreshore giving a good natural defensive position. The land on Loch Fyneside which has long been known as MacEwan country lies between the Kilfinan burn and Largiemore.
>
> Castle MacEwan is identified on OS maps as Caisteal mhicEoghainn. The OS Name Book, compiled in 1862-77,

gives as authorities the Old Statistical Account and Origins' Parochialist which record that it was the stronghold of the MacEwan's, former lords of the Otter. There is another stronghold associated with the MacEwan's, a mote-like structure known as Croc mhicEoghainn near the present Ballimore house.

The MacEwan's are descended from Aedh Anradham who married an heiress of Cowal and Knapdale in the eleventh century.

These old accounts can be a bit boring; I promise I'll try not to show any more of them.

The weather forecast was reasonably good so the decision was made; go for it. Our basic itinerary; Bed and breakfast in the Kilfinnan Hotel, a safari into the wild to find and explore the McEwan Castle then a week in the Oban Bay Hotel to explore the local castles.

On the map it looked straight forward enough, car drive to Gourock, Ferry across the River Clyde to Dunoon, coffee and a roll in bacon in the cafe on the shores of the Holly Loch then a drive across to Otter Ferry. Finally, down the coast to the Kilfinnan Hotel, find the castle, pay our respects, spend the night in the hotel and bobs yere uncle, off to one of my favourite places; Oban.

Plans of "Mice and Men" as they say; terrific journey on the M8 the by-pass from the busy streets of Glasgow, which by the way has a large connection with the Ewing family. A James Ewing at one time one of the richest men in Scotland owned a very large part of the land Glasgow City is built on.

On to the A78 which runs alongside the Firth of Clyde, great view of the Dumbarton Rock on the opposite shore. The memories this run brings back are fantastic, Margaret and I sailed down this river 56 years ago on the way to Ireland on our honeymoon. I also sailed it as a child on an old paddle steamer going to the resorts of Rothsay and Dunoon.

Great memories, and I remember what it was like before this motorway, a nightmare, although even now pick your time, during peak traffic hours it can be very busy.

Into Gourock and onto the car-ferry. I was parked beside an enormous lorry. It's time they got a bigger boat, this one is so low in the water, you get the feeling a big wave would sink the bloody thing and drown the lot of us.

Back on terra-firma, landed only a few miles from Dunoon then on to our first pit-stop. The Holly Loch; once regarded as the Little America of Scotland. Twenty years ago, with their heavy security I wouldn't have got within twenty miles of the place. This was where the Americans had had their submarine base.

Here I was having a bacon sandwich and a cup of coffee right where the Yanks had been for thirty years. Point of interest; I was an Engineer in Ravenscraig Steelworks and worked on the plant which produced the steel for the construction of our own nuclear submarines. I visited the plant where a sub was being constructed, it was unbelievably enormous, how they managed to get the thing back up off the bottom of the ocean, unbelievable.

This base at the Holy Loch had been an arsenal of nuclear weapons for the Americans, sufficient to destroy Britain and Scotland's most populated area is just 10 miles away.

Sitting in that little cafe and looking out over the Loch brought to mind an article I read recently and again my imagination ran away with me. In 1974 an American nuclear submarine armed with 16 Poseidon nuclear missiles left the Holy Loch on one of its missions and not far from the coast collided with a Russian similar type submarine. Fortunately, it was a scraping collision rather than a head on.

This near miss was of course kept secret until recently and seemingly the collision was a few inches away from being a major disaster. It happened only a few miles from where I was sitting and 30 miles from Glasgow my hometown, at this distance a nuclear explosion would have levelled the area and killed millions of people. Along with nuclear fallout an underwater explosion of such magnitude would have caused a Tsunami which would have swept everything in front of it right across the central belt of Scotland. There would have been no doubt retaliatory measures which would have ended up with the world at war. Certainly, it would have been the war to end all wars.

And Britain itself has a similar arsenal base only a few miles away at Faslane.

Don't get me wrong, I have many friends from America, in fact I have many distant cousins proven on the DNA project. I only wish our Politicians could agree to disarm these horrible weapons. OK enough of that stuff just let's say the taxi drivers and local entrepreneurs made a fortune when the Yanks were at the Holy Loch.

Another point of interest; the Americans were very disciplined and respectful to the locals and fair made themselves at home; so much so they actually had a tartan made and called it the Polaris Tartan. They probably knew they were descended from Scots.

On the road again, (nice pun, Johnny Cash) onto the B836 road heading for Otter Ferry. Big mistake; A bloody nightmare; a road only broad enough to take one car with ditches either side which would burst an axle if you drifted into them. Its surface was torn away and badly needed resurfacing, you could actually hear it tearing the tyres. We were dreading the thought of an on oncoming car or worse a lorry. The overtaking in-shots were few and far between and having to pass one another would have been near enough impossible. What looked like puddles turned out to be potholes some of which must have been full of manure, the stink was still in the car days after. If I had had room to turn the car and go back, I would have done so. Turned a blind corner and we were suddenly on a 45-degree hill in an enormous pothole. I'm pretty sure the front of the car was down on its axles, the car stalled. It would have been a bit of an experience being stuck in the middle of nowhere miles from civilisation with our mobile phones out of range.

Believe me I was worried, this wasn't one of those big four wheeled drive Jeeps, mine was a family saloon, a Ford Mondeo, a reliable car but not built for these conditions. After a bit of jumping up and down with back and forward persuasion I managed to reverse out and in first gear swerved around the hole and got up the hill.

I was a bit more cautious after that, 20mph was my limit and all eyes were focussed on those blind corners and hidden puddled potholes that's for sure.

Later we discovered locals do not use the road and prefer to travel an extra thirty miles because of its disrepair. According to reports the road has been destroyed by lorries which transport wood from the forestry and repairs to the road would bring the forestry work to a standstill. It is dangerous to motorists and thank god we did not meet a lorry. Word of warning to travellers "Stay off this road".

When we hit Otter Ferry that was us on what had been McEwan land, we were still on a one-way road but this stretch was in better condition, but not perfect.

After a few miles there it was the sign Kilfinnan Hotel, barely visible amongst the undergrowth. What a relief, we had made it but the worry now was; has the car been damaged.

The building looked to be a few hundred years old and it reminded me of the old horror movies, you know; the Adams family type. It was no surprise to hear the front door creaking, it was certainly eerie in fact I expected to see Lurch from the Addams family inviting us in?

Morticia and Gomez weren't at the reception desk it was a very helpful and friendly lady who introduced herself as Mandolin and showed us to our room.

Of course, I was letting my imagination run away with me again, inside the hotel wasn't too bad, even although it was old fashioned, quaint, and very quiet. I will not go into our trials and tribulations when we discovered we had forgot the keys to our suitcases, a bit embarrassing asking for help. Ended up bursting the locks.

The room was basic but fine, once settled in we went downstairs. In the lounge were a young couple playing cards. Seemed strange until they told us there was no Wi Fi or mobile phone signals, even the telly was a no-no; it had the bad reception rolling screen syndrome which civilisation had got rid of thirty years ago. The place was otherwise deserted, certainly if you want isolation to get away from it all and have a bit of peace and quiet this is the place. By the way Kilfinnan is so insignificant that most maps don't even show it.

We found it difficult to get to; what would it have been like six centuries ago? It would have been impossible for the McEwan's to travel inland, that horrible road would have been non-existent and those trees that are now being chopped would have been as thick as grass. Thus, the reason for most living areas being close to the sea. All travels and communication were done by sea. Loch Fyne would have been a pretty busy place that's for sure.

Anyway, we were here in Kilfinnan for one reason to visit the site where the Castle McEwan once stood, so with a bit of bravado and as the weather looked good, we decided to go for it before dinner.

Mandolin our hotelier was very helpful gave us directions and all sorts of advice. She also gave us a hiking pole and offered the use of knee-high wellies which we were stupid enough to refuse. I had on heavy walking shoes and Margaret ankle high wellies which proved to be totally insufficient.

We walked a half mile down the lonely not a soul in sight road to the Old Mill, strange looking place.

I don't know how that Mill ever turned its wheel the river was a good hundred yards away.

Now it becomes interesting; a large barking hound came bounding towards us, fortunately a woman shouted it off. Just as well; the beast could have ended up with a walking pole up its jacksie. The kindly lady gave us directions; "through the fields and head for the coast-line, remember and close the gates after you and keep to the fences the farmer doesn't allow the fields to be crossed".

I couldn't believe it beyond the first gate was an unkempt field; no path. The area was a minefield of cow-pats, cattle hoof prints and swamp. To crown it all; the bulls that created the mess were in the field. Can you imagine it? two old age pensioners in their late 70s and we were actually going ahead, if the bulls had decided to have a run at us, we would have had no chance. We were ankle deep in muck and searching for harder ground. The bulls were looking at us as if we were crazy, in this case they would not be far from the truth. Thankfully after following us for a mile or two they decided we weren't a threat and they went their ways.

After about an hour of plodding and still no path we came to a burn and a ton weight of a gate which had to be lifted as well as pushed. The burn had plenty water flowing and we had to paddle through it, Margaret was fair enjoying herself. By this time both of us had soaking plates of meat (feet) I tried to put a bit of cheer into our trip by singing It's a wonderful world, Margaret told me to shut up.

At last we could see Loch Fyne we could have done with some extra kit, a boat, a ladder and two pair of fisherman's waders came to mind.

After about a mile and another splash through burn we reached the loch and lo and behold there was a sign pointing along the shore - CASTLE McEWAN-.so at least we on the right path. Wrong saying there were still no paths.

The walk along the shore was quite pleasant, at last a bit of luck the tide was out. picked up a piece of pebble for a souvenir. Margaret was quiet, I suggested we go in for a paddle, she was not amused. It was my birthday after all. Low and behold another sign and another heavy gate,

We could see our objective; high ground maybe half a mile away. The only problem was what was ahead of us, a forest of jaggy bramble bushes. What the hell; we've come this far there was no way we were turning back. What we needed was even more kit; two large jungle clearing knives, protective leather suits and gloves.

I think the McEwan ghosts were putting these hazards in front of us; testing us, they certainly weren't making it easy and there was worse to come. After getting through the jungle and reaching a bit of a clearing we could see what was ahead. a steep face about 30ft high littered with very large boulders, it was the only way up. On one side was the sea on the other a large impossible to get through swamp.

This was pretty impressive as a fortification against intruders, it was obvious these need a crane to lift boulders had been placed in such a way to make it very difficult for men and impossible for horse to climb. To my mind this had been the start of their defensive set up, at the top there would have been a wooden rampart which was a common set up during the Roman times in Britain and that goes back a thousand years. And these large stones which were said to have been part of the castle in my opinion were never a part of any building.

I would have loved to have become involved in an archaeological dig on the site. It's obvious there is a lot more finds in the area and no doubt I would have had many an argument with them. All good fun.

I kid you not, there was no other way to get to the top it had to be climbed. Margaret refused point blank, whereas this brave little fellow took his life into his hands and with great effort managed to get to the top. I could see the cairn which signified the castle site the only problem was I had what looked like another jungle of very jaggy bramble bushes and nettles in front of me. In trying to avoid them I lost my bearing; Margaret was shouting I was shouting we had lost sight of one another and the bloody rain came on. Yet another piece of kit required, a couple of Large gale-proof umbrellas.

I reached the area, soaked, scratched and stung. A fantastic view of Loch Fyne a plaque on a five-foot-high cairn and wind and rain. I suppose I should have been glad of reaching it and have danced about naked; sorry I was soaked to the skin and it was running down my back. I can always say though; I have done it. Tried to take a few selfies, they didn't come out to well. Margaret was down below still out of site and near enough screaming rather than shouting and I was lost in the bloody jungle. Keep shouting Margaret I'll come to you it was my only way of getting back to my safe point of descent. Another piece of kit came to mind: a bloody compass and the rain was lashing down.

I discovered later that there was an easier access to the site, we had taken the wrong route.

It's said most old Castles are haunted, I never believed any of it. But this experience had me concerned. Were the ghosts of the McEwan's giving me a hard time, were they perpetrating revenge on me. Are they connecting me to a presumed former traitor? Yes, there could have been a traitor, the way I see it, for one of our own to have been in the pay of the Campbells when the Clans were the bitterest of enemies is unforgivable. A namesake of mine a William Ewing served them as a Servitor (Sheriff). A pretty high-ranking position.

There was certainly a lot of killing done in this area all those years ago and this place gives me the creeps. I expected a big ugly axe yielding highlander to run at me out of the mist. Believe me, this place has a haunted feel about it and not for the wimps like me. Another piece of kit comes to mind, a Ghostbuster gun.

I better get back to the hotel I'm beginning to let my imagination run away with me again.

The return walk through the boggy fields was even worse, the rain was pouring down the muck was getting deeper and the burns were flowing faster. Strangely the bulls had a look at us and ran away, we spooked them.... boom-boom.

When we arrived at the hotel it was hot showers and complete change of clothes. There was a large fire in the Lounge, very cosy. We had a nice meal and although exhausted got little sleep. My nightmare was horrendous, the McEwan's were cutting strips off me and roasting them on an open fire. No, they couldn't have been cannibals, surely not, anyway I refrained from eating meat for a few weeks after that. I got no reply just a hysterical look from Margaret when I suggested we camp out on the McEwan Castle site for a few nights.

Archaeological work at the ruins of the castle seemingly discovered along with some artefacts, evidence of a wooden structured fort which they said had been fortified with the stones from the castle. I tend to think there was never a stone-built castle on the site. There was no sign whatsoever of a foundation, not one stone of evidence. I would tend to think that this was a fort. The large stones I witnessed were in no way from a building, they were irregular clumps with no flat surface.

As was the case in those medieval days it was a worldwide feature for tribes to attack one another to gain land for their expanding populations. The Clans of Scotland were no different, I suppose it would be the case that the Campbells carried out the massacre of the McEwan's knowing if they didn't it would eventually happen to them. The Campbells certainly done the dirty on their guests, inviting them to a feast, filling then full of drink, giving them a good time, plenty to eat, ladies to entertain then the coup-de-gras. When the McEwan's were so intoxicated and they could not retaliate their throats were cut, everyone including the chief were slaughtered.

The cut-throats would not have been long in sailing down Loch Fyne and succeeding in the massacring of the sleeping men women and children occupants of Castle or Fort McEwan. They totally destroyed the place then routed the people from the land of the Otter. Those who escaped the evil murdering swords obtained sanctuary with the McLachlan clan or across the water in Ireland.

The Campbells had a reputation for befriending their neighbours then murdering them, they done the same a few centuries later to the McLachlan's and McDonalds.

The Campbells would not have put on record that they had committed murder, they put on record that the land had been gained legally, that the McEwan's had run up so much dept they had to forfeit their land to repay it. It's a case of what you believe, I cannot believe the McEwan's would give up their homes so easily, it's obvious that the massacre was what really happened and as has been proven so many times history was written as per the Lordships instructions.

The McEwan's although without a land, still managed to maintain a Clan and to this day they have a chief. In fact, I was introduced to him once. I and believe it or not bought him a pint of Lager. It was years ago where John Thor Ewing who I also met was voted to be the future chief of the Ewing clan at the inauguration of the Ewing Clan in Glasgow. I will describe a bit more about that historic meeting later.

We said our goodbyes to our hotelier Mandolin, she wasn't amused when I asked her if anyone had got lost and never come back from visiting the castle.

If you would not be forgotten.

as soon as you are dead and rotten.

Either write things worthy of reading.

Or do things worthy of writing.

Benjamin Franklin.

# Chapter 2.

## Our Beautiful Homeland.

Our next stop Otter Ferry, it was a tree on either side journey, a bit boring, fought off the sleep by listening to some James Last numbers. Not to worry it was worth it there was a place to get a coffee right on the shore-line, very nice.

Just sitting there soaking in the fresh sea air and admiring the view, that's what life is all about. The imagination can really run riot? There are the ruins of the McLachlan Castle on the Ferry's shore-line where I'll bet many a clansman had fought and died.

It is understandable anyone wishing to own this territory, it is absolutely beautiful. The scenery is outstanding and its position would have been ideal for the protection of shipping coming up the loch to Inverary. Ideal haunting area for all those generations of big hairy legged McEwan's who passed this way all those centuries ago. There are lots of mausoleums and grave sites. No Ewing's I'm afraid; Yes, Otter Ferry is a Painters and Photographers heaven I hope to be back soon.

Here's the strangest of coincidences: My older brother loved the area of Loch Fyne, of all the lochs and rivers to choose from, Loch Fyne was George's favourite. He had a Caravan on a Site just up the coast at Inveraray and many a weekend was spent on its shores doing his favourite thing, not knowing his fore fathers had done the same all those centuries before. I'm not claiming there was a bit of the supernatural about it. Then again, maybe I am. I had a bizarre experience myself once. I bought one of those do-it-yourself thingies for trimming the hair. You should have seen the mess; bald bits and tufts were the order of the day. I looked into the hall mirror which had been up there for Nye on thirty years and it fell off the wall. Honestly - true.

My younger sister Pamela swears there are ghosts and believes they can show themselves under extreme circumstances. My eerie experiences at the McEwan's and McLachlan Castle's makes me wonder?

McLachlan's were staunch Jacobite's, supporting Viscount Dundee at the Battle of Kiliecrankie in 1689, James VIII in the 1715 Uprising and again in support of Prince Charles Edward Stuart in 1745. The MacLachlan chief was at the head of his clansmen at Culloden in 1746 and lost his life in the cannon fire. His son was also killed in the battle. News of the chief's death is said to have been broken at Strathlachlan (Otter Ferry) when his riderless horse came home

Retribution after the Uprising by the English supporting Campbell's resulted in Castle Lachlan being left as a ruin. The estates were forfeited but later returned (thanks to the intervention of the Duke of Argyll).

We know from historical documentation that the McEwan's were part of the MacLachlan Clan they no doubt fought and died with the McLachlan's at the defence of their castle and alongside them at Killicrankie and Culloden.

This is another thing about the Ewing's that bothers me, they were staunch Presbyterian Protestants as far back as I can get yet most of the Clans were Jacobite and Catholic. Is it possible the Ewing's were on the opposing side supporting the English? God forbids.

Anyway, let's be on our way. We are now onto a decent stretch of road the A185, with the car still smelling it's into Strachur. A nice quiet quaint little village with it's made from recycled plastic jetty. No doubt Rev William Ewing was an enthusiastic yachts-man when he was a minister here during the $19^{th}$ Century.

Still on the road following the banks of Loch Fyne we reach the village of Cairndow, just short of the Head of Loch Fyne. This small stretch of road around the Loch has reputedly the most beautiful scenery in Scotland. Looking down towards the sea the sunsets are out of this world. There are high spots in this area where it is possible to view both Loch Fyne and Loch Lomond due to their close proximity.

A couple of miles and were in Inveraray, still on the land of my forefathers? This is one of my favourite places. We have often stayed in the Loch Fyne Hotel which overlooks the Loch. The town is famous for two things; the old jail and of course it's castle. Appropriate is it not, home of the Campbells with a jail to lock up their dissenters.

This is predominately the land of Campbell and it shows. It is obvious when one visits the so called Inveraray Castle, the home of the Campbells. What a place; certainly, showing how the other half lived. The building is enormous its inside comparable with a royal residence. Muskets, Lances, Swords and

Portraits of previous dukes of Argyle hang on the walls. Beautiful old-fashioned furniture in every carpeted room, carvings and tapestries adorn, absolutely disgustingly luxurious. And guess what? The castle has not only one but many ghosts, the sound of a Kiltie playing a harp, supposedly a young lad who had been murdered by the Jacobite's and a troop of red-coats.

I felt I had been swindled, we paid £10 each to get in, this wasn't ruins, this was but a replica of a castle built for someone who was worth a bob or two. It certainly showed us who had been the top dogs over the centuries. This lot were no doubt aristocracy who had the influence and power to write their own version of history. If only the truth could be known.

About 10miles east of Inveraray are the ruins of a castle called Innes-Chonnel, it sits on an island on Loch Awe close to a village called Dalavitch. It was the original base of the Campbells and how they came about owning it is anybody's guess. The castle has close connections to the McLachlan clan and probably the McEwan's.

I did mention that my older brother George was an ardent fisherman and had a caravan at Inveraray which was his favourite place before knowing Loch Fyne was his ancestor's area. Yes, Loch Fyne is even haunted? It has been seen on occasion, A medieval sailing ship, we'll not go into that.

Well my younger brother Eric under similar circumstances told me specifically that his ashes were to be put into the centre of Loch Awe. It's only a few miles from Loch Fyne. A sombre task which Margaret and I carried out.

Honestly, I do not believe in the supernatural, but why is it before I and my brothers knew anything about our family history we had been so attracted to this little part of Scotland.?

It was only recently I discovered that the Campbells were very much involved in the slave trade and owned plantations in Jamaica and other parts of the world. Coincidentally they were responsible for having transported prisoners from Inveraray jail to foreign countries, probably their plantations. On Inveraray prison records there are two Ewing children whose crimes were trivial, they probably were starving, stole bread and were sentenced to be deported. I had a good mind to ask for my £20 back.

Onto the A819 again fantastic scenery, I have never tired of travelling through these Glens, they are simply awesome.

Right on the head of Loch Awe is a little place called Dalmally and here again the Campbells are prominent. They built Kilchurn castle wae back in the 15th Century, it's just walking distance from the village, and I must admit these are must see ruins in a stunning setting, sitting on a piece of land which was once an Island and surrounded by hills and glens. The castle is also famous for playing its part in the television series Outlander. Get your boots on and get trekking this is worth a visit believe me.

Off again onto the A85, Ben Cruachan to our right where the impressive tunnelled power station is situated, again worth a visit. Through the villages of Taynuilt, Connel and Dunbeg then the famous city of Oban. It has been a journey I rate as one of the most scenic in the world. Even in the rain looking down from the mountains onto the lochs and glens the view is awesome. I had the Royal Scots Dragoon Guards tape playing as we travelled. Amazing Grace on the Bag-Pipes was a RSDG number one hit a few years ago, I love it.

## Chapter 3.

## A Kinsman in Dunstaffanage

Oban sits on the shores of a natural harbour looking over the sea to the Island of Mull, it is a major tourist attraction and has a large Ferry Port for sails to the Western Isles. One can have a short boat trip to the picturesque island of Kerrera and visit the Gylen Castle, in 1647 it was attacked and even though the resident McDougall's surrendered they were all slaughtered by the Covenanters (Ewing's were Covenanters). Like all other castles it must surely be haunted, the ghosts would certainly get peace and quiet, there are only about 50 people living on the Island.

There are many shipwrecks around the shores of Oban and its waters are favourite for underwater treasure hunters. It is recorded that a Spanish Galleon laden with gold sunk close by. Why it was on the Atlantic Ocean is a mystery? Maybe looking for America.

We have sailed on the Oban ferry to the Island of Mull on many occasions, the boat is spacious and very comfortable and a bite of lunch can be had while enjoying the fantastic sea views. Paul McCartney has a farm on the Island of Mull and is famous for writing one of the best-selling singles of all time; Mull of Kintyre.

Oban Bay's horse-shoe shape is ideal as a strategic protection against high seas and enemy ships. In extreme weather it is abound with ships all shapes and sizes; the little Island of Kerrera acts like a gigantic harbour wall keeping the Atlantic Ocean at bay.

In wartime over the centuries it was used as a gathering and setting off point, in fact, during the second world war merchant ships heading for the USA commenced their perilous journey from Oban Bay. How those sailors done it? They would have known the peril's that lay ahead. I would rate them as the bravest of the brave, the sea was swarming with deadly Nazi U-Boats and they knew they were sitting ducks. There was no way if torpedoed they would have survived, I'll bet there were many a sailor who was glad to be back in Oban's safe waters.

Wars, battles, killing. Why has the human race always had to settle their differences by slaughtering one another? Throughout history the evidence is shown by ruins and memorials and non-more-so than the Castle, it makes obvious what must have taken place during its demise. The shattered walls have been bombarded with cannon balls or boulders and balls of fire hurled by giant sling-shots.

We must remember when visiting these sites that there were people, men, women and children being killed during the Castle's destruction and we should show a little respect to their memory.

Oban has one of Scotland's oldest Castles; Castle Dunollie which had a King Ewan (Christian name) around about 1300. We gave it a visit; this is more than likely the furthest back Ewan on record. I would be very surprised if there was any connection to the Ewing's.

What a position the Castle has; a perfect view over the whole bay of Oban, a perfect strategic defensive outlook and an ideal spot for one to use their imagination. I would have been an archer on the wall-walk doing my bit by hitting a few invaders when the cannon ball hit the wall below me. I didn't live to tell the tale. Everyone in the Castle was slaughtered.

Unfortunately, the present-day castle walls are supported by scaffolding and a large area too dangerous to enter. Worth a visit, the tour guide gives a very informative history lesson and was very helpful.

The Campbells again were involved in many attempts to gain the territory around Dunollie Castle and were as per the McLachlan Castle on record as being responsible for its destruction and of course Dunollie like any honest to goodness castle is haunted. A lone Piper plays his tune, especially when the wind is blowing through the trees. Listen very carefully and use your imagination?

We met a couple from California, blethered for about an hour, gave them a few tips, they were impressed with Scotland and pleased to be in a country which didn't have frequent earthquakes and forest fires. Gave them directions to one of Oban's highlights, a nice little coffee shop on the front it specialises in chocolate drinks.

About 3 miles down the road from Oban is Dunstaffanage Castle. It also goes way back to the $13^{th}$ Century and has been held since the $15^{th}$ Century by the Campbell Clan. How they managed to obtain this is anybody's guess. Not by fair means I'll bet.

In 1621 a namesake of mine William Ewing - proven by DNA kin - was Servitor to Campbell of Dunstaffanage - a Servitor was a high rank officer who served summonses. This is certainly a bit concerning, the Campbells had a certain reputation which I would rather have had my ancestors having no part. Then again; maybe he was there as a spy for the Jacobite's? One can only hope.

The castle is partially ruined and is open to the public. Of course, like most it is haunted, this time it's by the Ell-maid of Dunstaffnage. A rather mischievous little devil who can take many shapes, tipping sleepers from their beds, making classical thumps and footstep sounds in the corridors; What some people will say to bring in the visitors. then again use your imagination.

We didn't see the ghost but soaked up the nostalgia, it was certainly an interesting few hours definitely recommended.

On the road again; we decided to head for Stirling, the A85 to Crianlarich about twenty-five miles through glens and over mountains. A fantastic Scottish journey, past the northern shore of Loch Awe where we placed my brother Eric's ashes, then through Glen Lochy with the beautiful Ben Lui towering above us and on to the junction at Crianlarich where the decision has to be made.; Is it to be the A82 to Glasgow via Loch Lomond or the tourist route A85/84 to Stirling via Callander and Doune?

OK we'll head for castle country, it's the A85 as far as Lochearnhead, a bit longer journey but worth it, the scenery is astounding, this little village is a major tourist attraction, probably having as many hotels and Bed and Breakfast accommodations per head of population as any other place in Scotland.

No castles but some beautiful old buildings. An architect called G T Ewing built the St Angus's Chapel in 1885. His work is evident throughout the region, more so a few miles away in the village of St Fillans where he built Dundurn Parish Church along with many Villas.

As a child I was a great one for fantasizing, still am, a typical child after all. Brainwashed by watching movies about Ivanhoe, Robin Hood and all those legendary characters.

I remember my Rocking Horse. It had been passed down through generations and the saddle was well worn. I also had a wooden stick which had belonged to my grandfather with a shaped horse's head on the end of it. I ran all over the place with that bit of wood between my legs making clicking horsey noises kidding myself on I was a knight of the round-table.

Fantastic childhood memories, we all have them and in some cases, it only needs two or three words to refresh them. Did you see the film The Holy Grail? Monty Python's comedians kidded along that they were riding horses, their servants clip clopping with half coconuts. Hilarious stuff; all filmed at Doune Castle in Stirlingshire. Oh, how I loved my wooden horse, and this nonsense brought it all back.

Would you believe it? Life can be full of surprises. During the Holy Grail film, the narrator makes the statement "Sir Robin rode north through the dark Forest Ewing" Intrigued, I investigated this possible familial link. I didn't have any luck. But what I did discover was that in 1581 King James Vl authorised £300 to be spent on repairs to Doune Castle, and a master mason called Michael Ewing carried out the work. Present-day repairs are being carried out. However, it is not an Ewing carrying out the current work. Not to worry; my name is on the visitor's book.

And step back in amazement, not only has the castle been used for Monty Python it was also used extensively on the series Outlander, Game of Thrones and Ivanhoe.

The ghost of the castle is really special, our very own Mary Queen of Scots used the castle frequently. It is said she was exiled here before she lost her head and her ghost has been seen on occasions, headless I assume or maybe just her head singing "I aint got no body".

A little bit of nostalgia: Probably where I got the liking for working in the kitchen and it's the furthest back possible connection to Ewing's I discovered.

In the accounts of the Lord High Treasurer of Scotland 1503 appears:

**For Ewin the boy in the kitchen ane cote.**

This was payment for duties in the King's kitchen and would have been given only for a position of a highly-trusted individual, although maybe insignificant to some. I believe this little piece of information proves Ewing's were prominent and trusted within the hierarchy of the day. Also, on the accounts of 1540 a payment to an Adam Ewin, and in 1588 the treasurer paid out "anekok" on behalf of the king to a Sir Archibald Ewein. A Sir no less; a knight, again signifying the Ewing's were connected to nobility in those far off days.

Chapter 4.

Callander to Stirling.

Callander now here's a place? just a main street really, has a chip shop, a Christmas shop, a woollen-mill shop and of course a golf course. The town is famous like most in the region for its walks in the surrounding hills. The very popular Bracklinn Water Falls is one of the largest in Scotland and very much a tourist attraction. If it's the right time of the year you will witness a salmon leap; a fantastic feat from these amazing fish. If you are a fisherman this is the place; plenty of trout in the local river which runs through the town. I can vouch for that, I spent many a holiday camping in the area surviving on the fish, absolutely delicious.

I'm a fan of Glasgow Rangers the most famous football club in Scotland. In 1872 Callander had the distinction and honour of being the team which played against them in their first ever match. Not many people know that you know.

A few miles away is Loch Katrine, Glasgow's source of drinking water and a terrific cruise on the loch is there for the keen sailors.

Just to let you know I, right now, while writing this am having a little drink of Loch Katrine water, of course being a true Scot I've added a little Malt whiskey to it. That's another thing about getting older one gets thirstier.

Next stop the illustrious city of Stirling famous for its charity shops, shopping mall and its territorial barracks on the shore of the river Forth where

William (me) was taught how to fight for his queen and country by the TA Royal Engineers.

The famous Castle and Monument in memory of William Wallace are both distinctive landmarks and both can be seen on the Stirling skyline long before the city is reached.

Being a very popular city it's one helluva place to take a car, narrow roads and very busy during the tourist season, I strongly advise Park and Ride if visiting.

All kidding aside the town of Stirling is the Biggy. It has one of the largest Castles in Scotland and a history comparable if not better than any other. It had been the Royal Court for Scottish monarchs, many including Mary Queen of Scots were crowned behind its walls.

The marks of musket and cannon balls still show on its walls confirming the many invasions it withstood and it has changed hands more times than the Ryder Cup.

One of the last sieges was in 1746 when it was defended by English troops against Prince Charlie's Jacobite's. The siege was a major mistake by the Prince, he lost his advantage by spending valuable time which allowed the English to recoup.

Robert the Bruce has his statue at the site of the battle of Bannockburn, a must see.

The famous Stirling bridge built close to the site where Wallace slaughtered an English invading army, fantastic history. I could write a book about Stirling there is so much history. I'm afraid it wouldn't be worth my while there are already enough written by bestselling authors to fill a library.

Stirling must hold the record for the number of books and movies that have been produced relating to it. Even now a film is being produced. all great, but I don't think any will ever supersede my favourite, the classic "Tunes of Glory" which starred some great Scottish actors including Duncan Macrae.

I have covered only a few Castles so far on my journey and they were all fascinating but so insignificant in relation to Stirling's. This is simply the echelons, the top of the league complete and still occupied fortress in Scotland. Why it still stands today is obvious, its advantageous position with numerous cannon around its high walls made it almost unsurmountable. No wonder the hierarchy including many centuries of kings and queens made it their place of residence.

I do not wish to make a big thing about it? I in fact feel a little bit ashamed that kinsmen of mine belonged to this hypocritical upper-class. A William Ewing was born in the Castle 1625 as was his son Baron William Ewing in 1660. The Baron had quite a few children; Nathaniel, Henry, John, Joshua, Captain James, Samuel, Anne and William. (A Baron was a person responsible for looking after the monarch's land and strongholds). The family moved to County Londonderry Ireland for whatever reason? was it to escape the persecutions the Roman Catholic Church were imposing on Scotch Presbyterians? was it for some other devious English conspiratorial reason? I hate to think.

Members of this Ewing family were responsible for chartering a ship and along with many Ewing's emigrated to America, this was in 1727, the ship was called the Eagle Wing.

There is quite a bit of history about this little ship. The "Eagle Wing" is said to have been the first to attempt emigration from Groomsport in Ireland to the shores of America. History says that she began to ship Scots hither as early as 1635, and that in

September, 1636 she took 140, many of them Ewing's, and that for more than a hundred years she was ploughing the deeps, bearing first and last many thousands of the best blood to the American shores. Yes, these were the Pioneers initially responsible in what was to become the greatest country in the world.

A president of America is reputed to have stated.

"For heroism and service and for the part her passengers took in founding this government, the Eagle Wing shades the Mayflower into a speck on the horizon of the local history of New England."

I am sorry if I have finished my tour with that little bit of what might be regarded as boring statistical conjectural information. Just let it be appreciated that if I am correct this son of a coalminer is descended from if not Royalty then a very high aristocratic and influential family of Knights, Barons, Lords, Bishops and last but not least Generals.

This is of course partly conjectural and could be disputed, I would be interested to hear any comments. w.ewing421@btinternet.com

And by the way I in no way would have had my life any different. I have had a good life; I don't think I would have enjoyed it any better if I had been born with the preverbal silver spoon in my mouth.

On that little piece of interesting fantastic information, I will end my tour by having a meal (fish and chips) in a nice little Restaurant on the outskirts of Stirling. I hope you enjoyed the journey.

# PART TWO

## Chapter 5.

## Cousins

As I said earlier Genealogy is a fantastic science, not only is it the means of discovering family it is also a means of making new friends.

Many years ago, I joined a group called the "Clan Ewing of America" later to be called "The Ewing Family Association of America" and through the internet made friends with many of its members, two in particular became exceptional good friends, in fact we have been in contact for almost twenty years and have proved ourselves cousins. Karen and Dick Childs from Oregon USA and to have met them in person when they were on a tour of Britain was one of the highlights of my life.

I do not think they believed initially that we were way back cousins, they could not believe my findings. I did not blame them, what I was suggesting at the time could not be proved with documentation. I certainly have a lot to thank them for; their disbelieve had them send me a DNA kit. This caused a bit of hilarity with my family, my son Andrew suggested I take the samples from the cat's backside, I wonder what results would have come from that. Anyway, I sent in my saliva samples and personally I believed wrongly that the tests would be a waste of time.

The results were amazing; not only did it prove my relationship with Dick; It gave me a list of about fifty Ewing men with similar DNA. It proved my findings that Dick Childs mother, Ewing by birth was a distant relation of mine, our connection being prior to 1800. And that all on the DNA list, who said they were Scots Irish were in fact also kinsmen.

Most of the matches were from America, they probably having had an ancestor on the previously mentioned ship the Eagle Wing.

There were also a few on the list who seemed a bit out of place and deserved a bit of investigation. A Christian Orr Ewing and his cousin Sir Alexander Orr Ewing from Scotland; an exact match with me. Now this was a surprise; the Orr Ewing's were and still are a very distinguished family who can trace their Ancestors back to William Ewing 1595-1640 who had a charter of Auchmelon in 1621 and lived in Dunstaffnage, the castle I visited in Oban, Argyll.

Prior to having my DNA results I was under the impression that the royal and distinguished ancestral line of the Orr Ewing's had no connection to mine.

They say DNA does not lie, so what it tells us is that we are kin and have a common ancestor probably within the last 10-20 generations.

I am pretty sure my direct line ancestors came over to Scotland from Ireland in the early 1800s and had been in Ireland for a few generations. The connection between the Orr Ewing' and mine must have taken place in Ireland, which is most unlikely; I would therefore suggest the link must be before the Ewing's moved from Scotland to Ireland.

This was extremely interesting because I discovered my own direct line back to 1812 were all coalminers living in Scotland, whereas the Orr Ewing's line included high aristocracy, and were I assume, from England, where they had even been knighted and married into royalty.

The Orr Ewing's were also amongst the richest families in Scotland, having built amongst others a replica of a castle close to Killearn and financed the building of Killearn Church. Margaret and I done our nosy and visited the castle; we were literally thrown out of the grounds. The place was enormous and is now a school for bad kids, we were told it was unsafe; they could be violent. Yes, there was wealth within the Ewing's of that there is no doubt.

In the little village of Killearn close to the castle there is on the war memorial an Ewing who was killed during the First World War.

I was in contact with a Christian Orr Ewing for some time, we exchanged information and like myself he was surprised to know we were kinsmen.

Amongst other friends from America were committee members of the "Ewing Family Association" (EFA) who I met personally at a meeting in Glasgow. Beth Toscos, Jane Weippert and Karen Avery who helped me enormously with my research.

The meeting in Glasgow by the way was with Lord Lyons deputy where the EFA were putting forward a case for the inauguration of a Clan status for the Ewing's.

I find it very sad that I am the only Scottish member of the EFA, for some reason the Scots are not interested. The group has an outstanding membership in the USA all of whom contribute and stay in contact with one another. I would definitely recommend becoming a member.

## Chapter 6.

## The Battle of Langside.

History always follows the wealthy and the aristocracy; it is very unusual for the common five eight peasants to be mentioned in records. I therefore during my research had to associate my ancestors with their Lords and masters. With this in mind I regret having to pick out the goings on of a very rich and influential family.

The Lord Eglinton's, Montgomerie's mainly, were a typical have a ball at the expense of others wig wearing hypocrites who lived the life of extreme luxury, owning all the land, building themselves castle like homes and treating their tenants no better than slaves.

I'm not a communist or even a bigot. I just do not understand how an individual could live a life in extreme luxury at the expense of those who had to live in extreme poverty.

I believe it more than a coincidence the number of times an Earl or Lord Eglinton has come up in association with the Ewing's during my research. These high and mighties actually passed laws where a peasant became a serf where he was bonded and under duress to do his lordships bidding, exactly similar to a slave.

Anyway, lets diverse a little and let me tell you a story.

Away back in 1568 when Scotland was a Catholic Country in a place called Langside - which is just a stone throw from "Glasgow Rangers" football ground at Ibrox and Celtic's Stadium at Parkhead. The Catholics and the Protestants had a bit of a set to and a namesake of mine one William Ewing carried the flag for Mary Queen of Scots. William had been given the task of protecting her colours, a very responsible job. No doubt her majesty picked one of her bravest and honourable subjects.

The Queens army was under the command of Archibald Campbell and the Earl of Eglinton. The battle was a bit of a disaster, with poor Queen Mary getting her head chopped off and the Earl of Eglinton (the Ewing's Lord and master) getting jailed. Those of the Ewing's who survived had to do a runner and as a result of her defeat over 300 men lost their lives.

Conquerors on both sides were cruel buggers towards prisoners in those days - burning at the stake, boiling in oil, public gutting and all sorts of atrocities - so it would be understandable the defeated getting as far away as possible.

As I said I am a Glasgow Rangers supporter and have been to a few games when they were up against Celtic. It is certainly a coincidence that the Battle of Langside had been a Catholic against Protestant affair and the football teams close-bye were in the same vein.

At one memorable game where there were probably more spectators than there were warriors at Langside I witnessed hatred beyond belief and vowed never to attend a meeting between the sides again.

As I said the Battle took place a few miles from the stadium, Catholic against Protestant, and the religious battle has never ceased. To this day they are still at it and it is nowhere more relevant than at the Parkhead and Ibrox stadiums.

Of course, there are fanatics on both sides, there always will be. Unfortunately, hatred is a human trend.

Enough of that, I watch the kicky-baw on the telly its safer, golf is my favourite sport, over the years I became quite good at it, in fact reached a respectable seven handicap and won a few medals.

I came across this little piece of history; Mary Queen of Scots enjoyed a game of golf. She played a round at the wonderful St Andrews and it is reputed she had her Cadets (servants) carry her clubs. Over the years, the term Cadets evolved to the present-day Caddies.

I played a round on the famous St Andrews Course, but I couldn't afford a Caddy. To the delight of a busload of Chinese spectators; with my first drive I almost hit a lady with a pram, I lost a ball, was in a few famous pot bunkers, bounced a ball off the famous Swilken Bridge and had a respectable score of 87. Celebrated by getting intoxicated and having a paddle along the shoreline.

After the Battle of Langside in 1568 where William Ewing had been flagbearer for Queen Mary, Lord Eglinton who had also supported Mary Queen of Scots was released from prison on the promise that he changed his allegiance from the Catholic queen to the Protestant king James.

He of course had no option and took part in many battles on the king's behalf. The retaliatory measures taken after these battles was ruthless slaughter and during the 16$^{th}$ and early 17$^{th}$ centuries king James with a determination to make Scotland and Ireland non-Catholic butchered thousands and dished out their land to his favourite Lords. Lord Eglington got a good share.

The Lord Eglinton's were the Lords and Masters over the population of a very large area on the west coast of Scotland from as far back as the fifteenth century right up to the early twentieth century. And my most certain information is that my gg grandfather Mathew as an infant came over to Scotland from Ireland in 1812 and in 1860 lived in a coalminers hovel owned by a Lord Eglinton in Kilwinning.

Mathew was but a serf to his Lord, he would have if not practically, theoretically, worn a slave's necklet with his owner's name upon it.

The Ewing's, as I said according to many historians were originally part of the Clan McEwan from the shores of Loch Fyne in Scotland and some it is assumed had to remove the 'Mc' from their name due to the bigotry shown towards Scots by the English and their supporters. They for some reason were stripped of their lands and therefore broke up and sought sanctuary. Many joined the MacLauchlan's while others went south into the territory of the Cunningham's.

During the 17th century the English monarchy was dishing out Irish land to their south of Scotland Protestant allies. I believe my ancestors received plots of this ill-gotten land from either the Cunningham's or the Montgomery's.

It is said that as many as forty thousand Protestant Scots moved to Ulster during the first ten years of the Plantation Program (this being the name given to the murderous clearances of Irish Catholic's by the English in their attempt to make Ireland a Protestant country).

A John Ewing was given land in Donegal County in 1614 and the family are still in possession. A point of interest is that the Cunningham's were very influential in Donegal during this time even having areas named after them.

According to my research my ancestors have been Presbyterian since its inauguration in the 16th Century and were Catholic prior to that.

It has to be appreciated how many Ewing family descendants John Ewing has had. In early days it was common to have very large families especially in the Catholic religion where contraception was disallowed, my discoveries show that my lot continued to follow the catholic trend. So, it is not inconceivable to suggest that around about 1,800 descendants could have come from this man alone over the last 400 years.

As part of the same colonization program, settlement was made at Plymouth in the Massachusetts-Bay Colony of America. This was the initial stage of the white man developing and settling the territory. There is no doubt Ewing's were involved even at this early date in the pioneering days of the USA.

In fact, it is on record that Ewing's were always there or there about. Think about it: if you name a place after someone, he must have either discovered it or initiated its settlement. What am I getting at? There are villages and towns all over America called Ewing, there's one in Nebraska, in Michigan, in Illinois, in Virginia, in Missouri, in Kentucky, and in New Jersey. Also, there's an Ewingsville in Pennsylvania. There are countless streets universities and even an Island off Cape Collier and that's America. In fact, we have Ewing's all over the world.

There are records which prove my kinsmen were pioneers of North America including Canada, that they were involved in the opening up of the west, and that they fought in battles against the British for independence.

In the *Biographical Dictionary of Early Virginia, 1607-1660*, Ralph Ewens, Esq, of London, England, is listed as an Adventurer in 1610 and 1620; Richard Ewins is mentioned in a 1625 James City County Court case; John Ewins is listed as being arrested for disturbing the peace in 1626. For City County James and William Ewins are listed as residents. (Mis-spelling of names was very common the majority being unable to read or write).

These early adventurers were probably forcibly moved from their homelands and there is a lot to be said for their steadfastness in overcoming the severe hardships they had to endure. Remember these were the days of the musket and sword in the wilderness of wolf, bears and Indians. Believe me; I am completely overwhelmed with admiration and humbly honoured to think that I may have descended from people such as these.

## Chapter 7

## Avoiding Death.

The sixteenth century, a time when Scotland was a virtual killing ground. Along with the hundreds of skirmishes between Clans at this time as many as 10 major battles took place in Scotland. Lords, Kings, Queens and umpteen different religious sects were all battling it out for supremacy. There were ghosts cropping up everywhere, castles being attacked and destroyed leaving headless ghouls, knights on white horses, white ladies and of course gigantic hairy legged highlanders appropriately dressed swinging large claymores or playing the bag-pipes.

I have probably mentioned it many times that I believe the common run of the mill individual would not be mentioned in historical documentation. The same goes for listings of recorded family trees, especially prior to the 18$^{th}$ century. To have discovered my family name this far back in time proves to me they were mainly very important people.

To prove a point; A James Ewing was a Burgess of Aberdeen in 1574 as was an Alexander Ewing in 1575. There is also record of a John Ewing living in Aberdeen at this time. There is a black side to this, the town which lies on the North East coast of Scotland had a bad reputation of being a refuge for Pirates and corruption, it wouldn't therefore surprise me one little bit if the Ewing's of Aberdeen had been involved in some illegal practices.

The South West of Scotland mainly Ayrshire was more popular for our lot at that time, in fact there are still a considerable amount to this day. There is no doubt though that the Ewing's were dominant in the Lands of the Lord Eglington and Cunningham.

Another point is that Ewing's during the sixteenth century were in positions of authority and predominately loyal to their Monarchs. And there is no doubt the Ewing's and their followers were participants in most of the battles in Scotland.

One of the major battles was at Dunbar in 1650, where Oliver Cromwell's Parliamentarian's defeated the Covenanter Scottish army. Lord Eglington and the Ewing's were involved, both being ardent Covenanters. Over 3000 Scots were killed and 10,000 taken prisoner, these were force marched into England where many more died. Some were shipped off to slavery in foreign lands including the Americas.

It must have been a devastating and horrific time for ordinary people to have lived, not knowing when the Lordship's men would ride into their village with their Fiery Cross demanding they leave their families and risk being cut to pieces by some sword swinging armour-plated horse-riding knight.

All able-bodied had to take up arms and protect their freedom. I'm quite sure the lad living in his little But and Ben with his wife and kids wasn't the least bit interested in whether Mary or Elizabeth or James or Charlie, or anyone else for that matter, sat on the throne. No doubt the Ewing's were shrewd enough to be leaders of men and keep their noses clean by standing back alongside royalty watching the riffraff doing the dirty work. Even if on the losing side the royalty by swearing allegiance to the victor; saved their bacon.

There were many instances for Scots having to do a runner. For instance, when James was monarch over both Scotland and England during the late 1500s, raids by the Clans over the border were forbidden and anyone taking part was hanged on the spot. There had been a major problem at this time with deprivation in the Scottish Lowlands; poverty and disease were rampant and the clansmen in many cases had no option but to continue their illegal deeds. The retaliation of the king and his lords was in many cases total annihilation of some of the smaller Clans and, for the luckier ones, slavery. (Margaret, my wife suspects the Ewing's were sheep stealers and my on-the-neck birthmark is a hereditary rope mark from the hang-man's rope.)

It is quite probable that some of my kin still lived in MacLachlan territory during the 17$^{th}$ and 18$^{th}$ centuries, at which time they would have been staunch Jacobite's, supporting Viscount Dundee at the Battle of Killiecrankie in 1689, James VIII in the 1715 uprising and again in support of Prince Charles Edward Stuart in 1745. It is a fact that some of the Ewing's adhered, with disastrous results, to the cause of Prince Charles Edward Stuart, which terminated in a fatal battle at Culloden on April 27, 1746. That Charles, we know, was a Catholic; but he was a Scot and, from the Scotch standpoint, the rightful heir to the throne.

You will notice I stated that only some would have followed the Catholic standard. The comparatively few Ewing's who did join them were actuated more by motives of patriotism than by sentiments of religion.

It is also possible my ancestors who I believe were protestant fought against the Catholic Jacobite's. I will not go into that?

Things just seem to be so contradictory? I'm not making things easier either, going back and forward in time and repeating myself on a few occasions; just doing my best to prove a point.

In the 17th Century the Ewing's were popping up in positions of authority. In 1600, a Robert Ewing lived in Cumry. Patrick Ewing lived in Strathdee in 1605, and Robert Ewing was Servitor (Sheriff) to Lord Sempill in 1607.

Thomas Ewing was Servitor to the Earl of Mar. Further, a Thos Ewing was Master of Lardner and received 333 pounds for services during the King's visit.

All over Lowland Scotland were the Ewing's. The Christian names John, James, Samuel, William and Robert have gone back hundreds of years and sustained to the present day. They are prevalent in my own family tree.

A Patrick Ewing from Ladytown of Bonhill, Loch Lomond, was reputed to have been the top man in Ewing affairs during the Scottish Civil War. He had a leading role in Covenanter politics and fought with them at the Battle of Preston 1648.

And again, Ewing's were prominent at the skirmishes of Argyll's Rebellion of 1685. The Ewing's unfortunately were on the losing side in all three battles and repercussions were forthcoming. In fact, after Argyll's Rebellion an Ewing was executed and his six sons fled to Ireland.

My contribution to the story of the clans with regards to the Ewing's is; to put it mildly a drop in the ocean. There are literally thousands of instances where Ewing's were more than likely involved.

All those historical battles and whatever, I'm quite sure the Ewing's were there. Not only my 'gut feeling' but also reading between the lines and a lot of evidence makes me think as I suggested earlier, that my ancestors before 1800 were mainly soldiers and adventurers, maybe not by choice; but through necessity; the ravages and aftermaths of war then forcing them to go further afield.

Mel Gibson starred as William Wallace in that wonderful movie Braveheart. The film is a fine example of what life was like in those far off days. The battle scenes were fantastically realistic and I certainly would not have enjoyed being on the wrong end of that gigantic sword of Wallace's.

Wallace would have loved this little ditty:

King Edward of England with his invading army was marching through a Scottish Glen. A shout was heard from behind a nearby hill. 'Hi Lavvy Heid send over your best two Knights and I'll gie them a dooin.' Of course, the challenge was taken on, and the Knights heads were thrown over and came rolling down the hill.

'Is that the best you can do? send over ten of your best and ah'll cuff the lot.' Again, the challenge was taken. Nine heads came rolling down with the tenth now naked Knight coming at the rear screaming 'Your Highness they cheated there's two of them.'

There is no doubt that life was extremely difficult way back. If you think about it, the little guy was terrorised by the ruling class who were little better than gangsters. Whole communities were exterminated in both Scotland and Ireland because they were the wrong religion. At a whim, our so-called royalty could order the murder of women and children simply to prove their own dominance and to bring fear as a way of preventing retaliation.

On the other hand, the hierarchy and rich if on the defeated side were given an option; my pick of the bunch was the traitorous Lord Eglington as I said earlier who changed his allegiance from the Jacobite's to the English.

It certainly looks like after the battle of Langside we had Ewing's on both sides and, unfortunately, I believe my side of the family were probably on the side of the victorious English at Culloden.

Anyway; most Genealogist's will appreciate that information prior to the year 1800 is a bit conjectural and as I stated earlier documentation could be taken with a pinch of salt, being written as per the rulers of the land.

I bet I have so far given the sceptics something to talk about? Believe me you've a lot more coming, I have plenty more mischief up my sleeve.

## Chapter 8.

## Nostalgia Gartcosh.

William Skidmore Ewing, that's my name. Skidmore was my mother's maiden name, her's was the posh side of the family, lived in the middle class over the hill side of the village. Unfortunately; none of the toffee noses lived to discover that their ancestors were coal-miners from the black-country in, of all places England. Mother was a bit of a snob and would not have been pleased had she been alive to learn that her great grandfather had worked under-ground.

In those days the coalminer was regarded as nothing less than a good for nothing low-life. My father as was his father, grandfather and great grandfather were coalminers. They had no option it was go down the Pit or starve and I am proud of them.

I was born on the 6th of July 1941 in a little village called Gartcosh. Just a typical little Steel-works plant with all its workers housed around it. My mother's father Edward Henry Skidmore worked in the plant for over fifty years and during the war due to shortage of man-power two of his daughters worked alongside him.

1941, what a year; not only significant because it was when I appeared on this wonderful world. It was when the Americans were caught napping by the Japanese at Pearl Harbour.

In a horrible way Japan done Britain a favour; the USA immediately joined the war and kept the

Japanese busy in the middle east while the alias fought in Europe.

There were a lot of bombs being dropped in the Gartcosh area, the Germans were foolhardily bombing our cities instead of our airports and I had to spend a lot of my dummy sucking baby-time in one of those gas mask-cradles in an Air Raid Shelter at the bottom of the garden.

I remember being told that the area around where we lived was intentionally lit up during bombing raids. Fortunately for us most of the Germans didn't take the bait, they only dropped a few on us. Unfortunately for the people of Clydebank a few miles away they were hitting their targets. The place was destroyed and thousands were killed.

Dad was a member of the voluntary force which helped fight the fires and rescue trapped individuals at Clydebank. He would have experienced some horrific scenes, that's for sure. I was too young to have remembered anything about the war, my first recollection of my childhood was going to Primary school; sometimes hanging dangerously onto the back of the heavy-steel-carrying Lorries to get up the steep hill. It was a bit of a climb for ma wee legs getting from "Whitehill Terrace" to the School, uphill all the way. It wouldn't have been so tiring if I had been allowed the help of my "Gird and Cleek". The Steelworks in the village which was the main employment for the community and the workers spent a lot of their time making these toys for the kids.

I didn't like Primary School much, preferring to play wae ma Pals and my wee dog Nippy. I remember getting the belt a lot. Believe it or not? the women teachers were the cruellest, they certainly had discipline, giving six of the best for the simplest of offences. When the bell rang, I couldn't get out quick enough. If there were no challenges for a punch-up, it was a race to get out the gate where there he was wagging his tail waiting for me.

Punch-ups were a common thing after school and I had my share of them. Luckily, I had an older brother who used me as a punch-bag and taught me how to fight. I also learnt then that girls were not as nice as they were made out to be. I watched a few girl fights after school, my sister Irene had a glorious left hook and uppercut defence. Those were the days, many a bloody nose I went home with and always gave as much as I got.

It was a lot easier getting home, running down the hill with Nippy. Even after seventy years I can still remember that wee dog looking up at me and hoping for a clap and a hug.

After school everyone had their chores, mine was waiting for me. Mammy always had it ready: A big juicy Canadian apple for me and for ma daddy an ex-soldier's flask full of hot soup and an ex-army mess tin stuffed with sandwiches.

It was my job to take them along the road to the coalmine where he worked. I would meet him on the surface. He would be stripped to the waist and as black as the ace of spades, a Coalminer who made his living lying in a wet and filthy environment 200ft down, shovelling and howking all day. I sat with him, usually getting a titbit biscuit or a piece of cheese. Then back down into the darkness he went, turning and giving me a wave just before he and his carbide lamp were out of sight.

A memory which has lived with me all these years, I sure thought the world of my Old Man (father).

During my lifetime I have heard quite a number of strange and weird stories, one which I have never forgotten came from an old miner many years ago. According to him the cage came to the surface with an unconscious fireman on board. When he came round he was still in a state of shock and nervously said that he had been inspecting an abandoned part of the Mine when he saw a strange glow approaching. Within the glow was a crouched woman with a basket strapped to her back and head. In her arms was a small child which looked badly crushed. He said the woman was greatly distressed and seemed to be appealing to him for help, she disappeared into the side of the tunnel and he ran like hell for the cage to take him to the surface.

My father, Samuel Ewing, was a hardened collier, a father I loved and strived to live up to. If you would like some insights into what a collier family's life was like, watch the movie, How Green Was My Valley, it's certain to bring a tear to your eye. Or better still buy my previous book called "WHY". It's an eBook about myself being witness to a colliery disaster. It's on Amazon Kindle.

I loved my childhood. I had had the fortunate luck to have been born in Gartcosh, the little village had everything to give a boy a piece of Huckleberry-Finn adventure: a loch to sail rafts and swim in; an old Pit Bing to dig for coal and earn a few bob selling; a couple of farms and plenty of countryside and a lick your lips terrific ice cream and sweet shop. What more could one ask for?

As I said, I wasn't fond of school but there were some exciting times during my childhood. An exercise which started during the war, due to lack of manpower was to have the school putting the boys onto the farm to assist the farmer. We had some great times, building hay-stacks and lifting tatties. It was hard work but we had great fun. Not so great was when my older brother George smashed his hand while trying to kill a rat, not a pretty sight.

Our house was right next door to the Farm, and we spent a lot of time doing odd jobs for the farmer. I remember while walking through the Cowshed a cow coughed at the same time as having a bowel movement. I got the lot all over me, I swear those Cows were laughing at me.

These were the good old days. I would do anything to earn a few coppers. Dad was a bit of a business-minded person he had a thing going: making Briquettes from Pitch and dross from an old Pit Bing he owned. My brother George and I carted, on a pony the briquettes to Dad's customers who were very charitable with their tips. Another task was helping collect Broque (brown bin stuff, left-overs etc) for my pal's dad's pigs and guess what: I got three pence per pail of horse manure; I'll not go further into that. I even peeled tatties for the local chip shop. By the way, that's when they knew how to make good French-fries.

Another memory from all those many years ago, was packing a big trunk, getting on a train and going on holiday to Dunoon. The sail across the Clyde on that wonderful paddle-steamer the Waverly, watching those beautiful big steam-driven pistons in the heart of the boat was the thrill of my life.

We stayed in a Prefab with my mother's sister Irene which was close to the park where the local Highland Games were held. It was another highlight to our holiday; seeing the Cowal Games. What a sight; the whole town was crowded with excited kilted people, I'm afraid I haven't the hairy legs required for the kilt.

The memories, sitting on the grass banking, watching the kilties dancing to the music of the Pipe Bands, it all brings a smile to my face.

I remember it well, fantastic tingles to the spine stuff which inspired thoughts of Scottish castles, battles and kilted warriors. I must make a point of going to the Games again soon, maybe in 2019.

Little did my family know that a very wealthy entrepreneur and kinsman of ours was responsible for making Dunoon what it was; a very prominent holiday and tourist centre. James Ewing the Lord Provost and first MP for Glasgow in 1832.

He was one of the richest men in Scotland, responsible for many industrial projects and, like me, no doubt, fond of castles. He was responsible for building a replica of one in 1822, it is now a museum and sits on Dunoon's highest point overlooking the Pier and the sea.

Enough of that gobble-gook, back to me as a wain (child). I certainly was not born with a silver spoon in my mouth, that's for sure. The family didn't starve, when father was unemployed the family lived on snared rabbit or even a chicken or two.

I remember the family digging on the Pit Bing, rummaging for bits of coal just to keep the fire going. Happy days, not long after a family lost their child doing the same thing, he went to close to a burning patch and like quick-sand he sank in.

We had a family of toffs living in a mansion type house up the road whose kids went to private school and weren't allowed to play with the local riff-raff. They had a smashing orchard, pears, plums, apples the lot. Their six-foot wall with broken glass on top couldn't keep this little fruit lover out that's for sure. My incursions ended badly though. On my last visit to the garden, the local polis was waiting for me coming out; He cuffed my ear and dragged me home. Mammy was not pleased and gave me a good hiding. Dad was disappointed I had got caught.

Remember this was just a few years after the war, Food was rationed, soldiers were coming home and I was old enough to remember it.

Going to the movies was a regular occurrence, the pennies I made from all the jobs I had got us in with 2 ounces of soor-plooms. Charlie Chaplin was one of my favourites. For some horrible reason my main memories were of the Newsreels showing the atrocities carried out in the German Concentration Camps. To think this happened during my lifetime, man's inhumanity to man and it just highlighted what really happened during all those previous wars that took place in Ireland and Scotland.

For instance, the evil Highland clearance's saw the destruction of the clan system and was responsible for among other atrocities, the starvation and deaths of thousands. The Irish people were treated no differently, being literally slaughtered by the thousands and their lands handed over to traitorous Scottish and English Lords.

The Scots and Irish people suffered greatly under the heel of England over the centuries and there is no doubt this terrible suffering led to the mass emigration to lands all over the world.

The famine in Ireland in 1741 killed 400,000 people and it is said it was intentionally orchestrated by the English. I don't remember the movie but the scene sticks in my mind; the English soldiers herding the people into their local church, barricading them in and setting it on fire. The battles between the Irish Rebels and the British forces, including The Battle of Vinegar Hill in 1798, annihilated thousands more. The battles in Scotland that culminated with disaster at Culloden and the atrocities that followed all contributed to the thousands of Ulster-Scotch emigrating to America and off-course most of it was covered-up, the perpetrators writing their own history.

Yes, true, there were a lot of Ewing's who went the full hog and ventured into the wilds, but my direct line ancestors done the Dunkirk-hero thing and stayed behind to take the flak.

Unfortunately, my years as a wee laddie in Gartcosh went by too quickly, and to crown it all heartbreakingly, I lost my best four-legged pal Nippy. We had gone everywhere together, and I'm pretty sure, like me, he enjoyed the adventure. That little dog was my best pal and even slept alongside me. I buried him at one of our favourite spots. I have a tear in my eye right now thinking about him. They built a motorway over the spot. I remember him every time I drive over it.

Yes, that was my Gartcosh years, short and sweet, my primary school days were over, we were off to pastures new. The family moved to a new three bedroomed terraced house in Muirhead, Chryston, in 1953. The roads were not even tarmacked and we had to lay planks down to run the wheelbarrows of furniture into the house.

Point of interest: According to recently disclosed, secret wartime information. A Starfish Decoy position was also situated just along the road a bit from the Mine and Gartcosh. Weren't we lucky the Gerrie's didn't take the bait?

## Chapter 9.

## The Old Man.

You might think I'm jumping about a bit and repeating myself occasionally. Well it's like this, my way when writing is to imagine I am having a conversation, even maybe talking to myself? No-No don't be stupid it's in my mind, I may be getting a bit donnart (silly) in my old age well isn't that a trend? By the way; getting old is a nuisance, amongst other things I feel I have to fight against saying things I might regret? It can be embarrassing but it's one of the advantage's in writing; you can almost say what you like and not get a punch on the nose.

I hope my work so far has been of interest, I have covered quite a lot so far and have been doing my best. That first paragraph was really to confuse and impress on you the reader not to take me to seriously. Honestly, I am trying hard and just remember I am no Shakespeare, I am a retired 78-year old coal-miner re-editing for the umpteenth time a story I have been working on for over 20 years.

OK; Now I'm going to get right down to it; get into the serious stuff, maybe even make a few minor mistakes and have you the reader wondering what's coming next. Exactly what I'm after, keep guessing; it's good for the brain.

I've got over 600 years of family history to cover and I am going to do it. without boring you to tears. I'm starting with my father and going to work back in time to the year 1500. Yes, step back in amazement? I have discovered a direct line ancestor who was born in the year 1500, that's a lot of Grand Pappies to write about and a lot of history, I hope you enjoy it.

As I said earlier the Old Man (local term given to one's father) was a typical coal-miner. A strong hard man, built from hard work and beer. He moved from the Gartcosh coal-mine to Bedlay Colliery around about the year 1950. Bedlay; a colliery which became one of the most modern pits in Scotland; it eventually had all the latest mod com stuff of the day: mechanized self-advancing face lines, hydraulic operated coal cutting shearers, underground locomotives and even face line telephone communication.

I hold my head high with pride when I realize what my father achieved, starting as a regular Face worker shovelling coal every day to a top management position as an Oversman. He had studied and passed all the necessary papers to eventually be in total charge of the nightshift, responsible only to the Manager.

Dad (1909-1969) was married on Christmas day 1931 to my mother Florence Skidmore (1911-1986). They had six children Samuel, first child died very young (unknown), George (1934-1999), Irene (1938-2006), William (me) (1941-......), Eric (1943-2015) and Pamela (1947-......).

A word about my brother Samuel, I didn't know until I was told at my mother's funeral that he had existed; I searched and searched with no luck. No record of birth or death. It must have been a terrible time for them as throughout their lives they never spoke about it.

In those early years we didn't have Telly's, mobile phones or any of that rubbish. Life was spent outside in the living world. In fact, my first experience with a television set was on June 2, 1953, a very memorable day in fact. It was the day of my Queen's coronation.

Joe Alexander, our next-door neighbour had all the wains (children) of Drumsack-Avenue in his living room. Watching in awe that black-and-white rolling picture, we were as quiet as mice, totally amazed as we watched this amazing piece of technology. It still amazes me how that moving picture can be transferred to homes all over the world. And to think today's gadgets supersede Telly's. Way out of this nuts-and-bolts engineers league I'm afraid. Maybe wonderful inventions but I'm afraid they have ruined children's chances of a William Ewing-Gartcosh experience.

We had a cat named Booboo, an amazing animal who simply adored my father. It used to do the most incredible things. She actually knew somehow that it was time for him to come home from the Pit and meowed like a baby to get out to meet him. It sat on our gatepost staring up the street waiting for him to come into view and when he did, it was a sight to behold, let me tell you. That Cat would recognise him right away. She ran from about a hundred yards away, full skelter, and jump into his arms and ended up wrapped around his neck purring her heart out. Unbelievable stuff; the cat truly loved him that's for sure.

Even more spectacular was the occasion when the cat had kittens, Dad would be sitting on the Big Chair, (called that not because it was bigger than the rest but because it was his), and Booboo had to go out for her ablutions. She would carry all her offspring from the basket, put them in his lap, then come back later and put them back in their bed.

My father Samuel Ewing was a good man and that little cat called Booboo knew it, it could sense the caring affection and trusted him explicitly. Simply incredible.

My mother and father both kept in contact with their families. Dads were in the Baillieston area, quite a bicycle ride from Gartcosh and ma wee legs had to keep up wae ma big brother and sister. It was always worth it though. Dad's sister -my Aunt Lalla- would have a big pot oh soup ready and waiting. We also visited my Dad's cousin Geordie Forsyth who was the caretaker for the local Loch near Shotts.

Mam's family were in Dunoon, Gartcosh and Coatbridge, I remember walking to visit Aunt Dolly - my mother's sister - with my big sister Irene (Pet) in Coatbridge. One time, coming home, it was quite late, the Pub was coming out and this drunk exposed himself to Pet and I. When Pet reported this to Father, both he and George, my older brother, went out after the Flasher

When I saw them the next day, I asked what had happened. Their reply was "You don't want to know".

Yes, many memories, oh how I wish my ancestors had written about theirs.

Anyway; here's a little bit of interest to chew on.

In the *Records of Augusta County, Virginia*, it is recorded that Indians took prisoner a John Ewing. John, of Gallia County, Ohio, testified that he and Jane Clendenin were carried away on the day her father and her brothers and sisters were killed in Greenbrier, July 15, 1763. They were kept in the same nation, but not together, except on their journey to Pittsburgh, where they were freed May 14, 1765.

John was sixteen years old when he was taken a prisoner and Jane, who later married a Mr. Davis in 1774, was only five years old when she was taken.

This John Ewing spent almost two years a captive. How was he treated? The mind boggles. Did you see the film 'A Man Called Horse'? If young John got similar treatment from the Indians, he must have become a man pretty early.

I must mention my initiation, a past down the generations thing. It was done to my father and his father.

It happened just a few days after my seventeenth birthday, which was middle of July 1958. We stayed in a wee Cottage called Philomena in Greenfoot, a village located between Glenboig and Annathill.

It was a smashing morning and still early enough for the dew to be sparkling away on the cobwebs among the grasses, the old Skylarks and Blackies were singing their hearts out.

Yup it was a smashing day.

As per usual we got off the road and into the fields, that's where it's all about. It's just amazing the amount of wildlife we often came across. The Deer were rampant in the area as were rabbits, sparrow hawks and even on lucky occasions that famous bird which is and has been over the centuries a symbol for many countries; The wonderful Golden Eagle.

After a few miles we got to our favourite spot, there was no eagle this time but still a pleasurable walk. We were on a hill overlooking Bedlay Pit on the path between Mollinsburn and Annathill, not too nice in that direction but to the north was the beautiful Campsie Hills.

It was exhilarating sitting there blethering away, the 'Old Man' doing a bit of reminiscing and me listening intently. He talked about his brother George going to Canada during the big strike and how it upset his mother. How his mother died when he was only five and his father remarried; his times during the war when he was in the Special Police and done Fire Brigade duty during the Clydebank Blitz, the stories were coming out thick and fast.

It was obvious there were things troubling him; I could sense it.

He was the type who regarded passing on problems as a weakness, and being young at the time, I unfortunately really didn't appreciate he was, in a sort of between-the-lines way, reaching out for help.

Back then, the area was simply covered with mushrooms, small delightfully delicious little things. We ate them raw along with brambles and raspberries. A right Tinkers Picnic we had, that's for sure.

I often think back on those times and that particular spot. In fact, I wouldn't be in the least bit surprised if an archaeological dig in the area wouldn't disclose some big surprises. Don't laugh, there is an old Mausoleum close by and it looks as if they could have once formed a building, and there are a few graves in the area. Don't forget the Monks mined for coal there hundreds of years ago. Also, step back in amazement: The Roman Antonine Wall is only a few miles to the North.

We were just sitting there enjoying the scenery, when my Dad turned and gave me a little smirky glance, looked at his pocket watch and said in a quiet but definite tone: "Let's start for Mollinsburn, I'm going to buy you a Pint."

Those words were ecstasy; pure unadulterated bliss. Thoughts of Shangri-La and they will live with me forever. I was receiving my initiation, my first official drink in a Pub, and I was having it with my Dad. Simply terrific. I was in the drinking fraternity, no need to hide it anymore all legal and above board. I was no longer the child who had to wait outside; I could have a Pint in the Pub with my

'Old Man'. No kidding-it felt very, very good that day.

Going down that brae into Mollinsburn felt like I was floating, I recalled the many times I had to wait outside with my packet of crisps. All those times were gone, I was now an adult. I got into the Pub, up to the Bar, got my Pint and enjoyed it as bloody nectar, and I felt like a God.

By the way; Thank god the barman said nothing about me being a regular and I offered to buy a second round but Sammy (Dad) wouldn't hear of it.

Life can be a bitch at times; one of my most fearful experiences during my life-time was witnessing my father having a heart attack. He did survive, but my god he did suffer, I remember like it was yesterday. Looking back and remembering our initiation I can appreciate why he had his attack. All the worry he had, throwing all his savings into a deposit for a mortgage on a house which proved to be a bad-apple that was sinking into the moss.

Yes, Dad had been worried sick, so much so he almost died. I felt so guilty, he suffered so much that day and all I could do was watch. Thank God he survived; I would never have forgiven myself. It taught me a lesson, that's for sure. I joined the First Aid class the following week and got quite good at it actually, giving the kiss of life to the female blown up dummy was my class act. A very exhilarating and climatic experience by the way. Fortunately, I never needed to do it to a big, ugly coal-miner.

I could always talk to my 'Old Man'. We were the best of pals, it wasn't really an old-style father-and-son relationship; you know, one where you addressed your father as "Sir" and all that rubbish. Ours was a more congenial and friendly arrangement. I simply got a kick up the backside if I said or done anything out of turn.

He was a right character, that's for sure. Many a story could be told about Sammy Ewing, one of the old rough-and-tumble, hit-first-ask-questions-later coalminer stock.

And another point of interest he was friendly with the young Charles Gray who in his later years was knighted for his services as an MP.

Again, I say how I wish my father and his ancestors had written a little about themselves. I would have treasured the smallest bit of information. I know I was absolutely overwhelmed with delight when I discovered material about my connections in Ireland, again we'll come to that later.

Dad was a cowboy fan, weren't we all? John Wayne, hero of the West, his film Stagecoach was brilliant and had us all carrying toy pistols and wearing cowboy hats. Yes; father had his to? he could beat us all at the quickest draw.

I wonder what he would have said if he had known his ancestors had been involved in the opening up of the west.

I discovered a Ewing connection to Jesse James, a well-known gunslinger. I wonder? is that where dad got his fast action; yes; I believe some of our attributes are hereditary.

Robert Ewing Younger was, along with his brothers a member of the James–Younger gang, notorious bank robbers and ex-confederate soldiers who sought revenge for the murder by Union soldiers of the Younger's parents.

I researched a bit, looking into why Bob Younger would have the middle name of Ewing and although no proof of being kin, they had a connection through drink. Jesse James was shot by his cousin Robert Ford.

Otto Ewing, a saloon owner in Oklahoma City, where Jesse James was killed, was reputed to be party to the death of Red O'Kelly, the man who killed Ford. A lot of retribution took place, the gun being the final solution.

I would not be in the least surprised if there were Ewing's involved in these inter-related events. The James's and Youngers were descendants of Ulster-Scots as were the Ewing's, no doubt together doing the proverbial runner from Scotland to Ireland and eventually Missouri.

What an existence these guys had. It was rough, that's for sure.

Yes, the movies were exciting. But can you imagine the extra pleasure my family would have had had they known their ancestor cousins had actually been involved. Just picture it: an ancestor, maybe a great-great-uncle with his family - all alone in the wilderness, travelling to the west via Conestoga wagons or establishing a homestead - being attacked by half-naked painted, axe carrying scalp-hunting 'savages'. I would probably have been shooting arrows up at the screen instead of folded up bus tickets.

## Chapter 10.

## His Name Was George

I hadn't even known his Christian name, the man responsible for creating my father, I should think black burning shame of myself. I hope when in the afterlife if we meet, he will forgive and give me a little credit for bringing his and his ancestors memories into the land of the living.?
Finding him wasn't too difficult, in fact it was quite easy. I obtained a copy of my father's death certificate from my mother, then with the information from it and a few bob(shilling) investment with Ancestry.Co I obtained the information I required. Grand Father George Swan Ewing born 1867 in a mining village called Shotts.

Now this was a place, in George's day a thriving little industrial complex. Now sadly an insignificant hidden in the middle of no-where two or three rows of houses. It lies roughly midway between Glasgow and Edinburgh. During the 19th century it was renowned for its mining and ironworks and at one time there were 22 coal mines in the area. Nowadays though there are none, the main source of employment now being the local prison.

The past three or four generations of my family have had family links with the area and there are quite a few cousins hanging about even yet, not in the prison, I hope?

Shotts claim to fame is their Pipe Band, 15 times winners of the world championship. The band formed no doubt from mining stock over 100yrs ago as their initial rehearsing place was a kitchen in a miner's row. Pretty noisy for the rest of the residents I'll bet.

Kirk O Shotts (Church), if you believe and are interested in ghosts this is the place to visit. Reputed to be one of the most haunted places in Scotland; it sits on a high spot overlooking the M8 motorway and has the eeriest looking graveyard you are ever likely to see. Mysterious figures have been reported on many occasions and one of its main characters is a grey lady whose identity is unknown. It is said that thirty witches were burned at the stake here and on one occasion a passing driver hit a mysterious apparition which vanished into thin air. I'll bet the grey lady is one of the witches. Wooo-Ahhh.

It was 1879, Granddad George would have been twelve years of age when a serious cholera epidemic hit Scotland. where 1000s died. There is no doubt poor wages and appalling housing conditions were responsible. Streets with open drains where effluent and everything else was dumped, families were living on bread and water. The little respect shown to coalminers was obvious when the cholera's victims were buried in mass unmarked graves just next to their cottages. This happened at Crosshill in a local village called Baillieston.

Those were hard times and they persisted throughout my Grandparents lifetime and beyond. Life was cheap; the Mine-owners had the Tory Government, the Law, the Army and Religious factions on their side. The Collier was simply a Serf with no standing.

These were also the early years of confrontations between miners and management. It was common practice for bully-boy police and soldiers to hound the coalminers back to their work. Then there was the First World War, coal-miners luckily were exempt which, no doubt spared the lives of a few of my kinsmen although there were still many deaths occurring underground.

Life would have been very difficult of that there is no doubt and thankfully my Grand-parents lived through their generation and had a son who was my father. Thank-you George and Isabella.

I see George as having been a hard-working family man who lived with one objective in mind; to better himself and make life as pleasant as possible for his children.

He spent all of his working life in the coalmines of Lanarkshire in the vicinity of Baillieston and Bargeddie. This was certainly the time when the industrial revolution was at its height. There were thirty Pits in the area and all in the locality of the Monklands Canal; A brilliant feat of civil engineering; It opened in 1790 its sole purpose; to transport the coal in barges from the pits to the Iron-works. The famous James Watt supervised the construction of the canal and it was also his steam powered pump which made it possible to mine coal at untried watery depths.

In its heyday the Canal would have been crowded with horse drawn barges travelling bow to stern, carrying coal to the Iron Works in Gartsherrie. It was as I said a marvellous feat of Engineering, and Ewing's had a big hand in its construction. James Ewing of Glasgow invested a very large sum of money into the project.

Another marvellous feat of engineering constructed 200yrs later on the site where my father discovered his father dead is the Baillieston Motorway Interchange. I look on it as a memorial to my Grandfather and all the other miners who lived and died in the vicinity.

A man who had loved his family and while providing for them still managed to work his way into a position of responsibility in the Pit. He is on record as being an Oversman (manager).

Having had three wives; not at the same time of course also tells us he endured a lot. Losing a loved one twice, the thought of it is sufficient for me to shed many a tear. He was a hard man and could have told many tales, of that I'm sure.

The 1920s were to say the least a time of strife for the Miners. According to Winston Churchill they were enemies of the people, of course, he was part of a Tory government which despised the idea of workers having the right to fight for better conditions.

A state of emergency was declared when they went on strike and troops were deployed in Scotland and Wales. On first of May 1926 due to the fact Miners refused to accept lower wages and longer working hours. Collieries in Scotland were closed. Three days later the first General strike began in support of the Miners. The country came to a standstill, unfortunately pressure from the Government and betrayal of the TUC stopped the General strike. The Pits gates were still closed and the Miners were starved into submission.

Mr. James Ramsay, who once worked in the pits and the brickworks, said "You had to live through it to know what it was like." There was no work for a year and the men organised soup kitchens with a bit of bone from a friendly butcher and some vegetables from the nurseries. The Co-op gave you bread and tatties on tick if you were a good customer and the jam works sometimes provided jam. Children searched the Bings for scraps of coal tae heat the house.

The Pits were reopened in November and the employers enforced lower wages and longer working hours. Unemployment and poverty reigned and though some men were fortunate to find work outside the district many others were forced to emigrate.

There are few families in Baillieston today without relatives in the Americas. It may well have been the Second World War and the housing boom which followed that prevented the village of Baillieston from becoming just another derelict mining village. All the Pits were gone and very little industry left. One major thing to their credit; as I said earlier; "The community spirit was grand in those days. Folks helped each other out."

As I said the Mine owners had taken advantage during the strike with an iron fist. Going as far as to have children arrested for removing coal from the Slag Bing. They refused to employ the ringleaders of the strike and evicted them from their homes. Difficult times indeed; The Miners were 26 weeks and more without a wage and in the end humiliated into accepting the harsh conditions. Grandfather George and his family survived those terrible times, knowing the Ewing spirit, they had probably rustled a few sheep or poached a salmon or two.

While walking from his home at 7 Commonhead Road Bargeddie to his work he collapsed and died. Grandfather George had only been sixty years of age. It was on October 1$^{st}$ 1927 after a search my father found him at "The Grove" Easterhouse. He had been seventeen years younger than me and astonishingly his father, grandfather and his son, (my father) all died at the age of sixty.

In this day and age sixty is quite young; in those days it was an achievement for a coal-miner to live that long. Another remarkable coincidence; when I was sixty, I had a heart attack and only for medication I would have kicked the bucket, that's for sure.

I live not far from Easterhouse and Swinton, places grandfather had lived. I can remember them as a few rows of Miner's cottages with a railway and canal running through. Now he wouldn't know them, the grass fields have been built upon and overhead motorways criss-cross the place where he died.

The area in the sixties was actually over populated to an extent where anarchy prevailed and it got a bad name. Gang fights, robbery and violence were regular occurrences, the locals being literally housebound. It got a lot of nationwide publicity at the time; Frankie Vaughan the singer playing a part in cleaning up the gangs.

Being the brave lad that I am I visited the place, and apprehensively walked about a bit searching for the place where grand-father died "The Grove". All I found was a cul-de-sac in a private housing estate by that name. Being persistent eventually I got a bit of luck. Met a couple of old retired coalminer's who were only too willing to help. Although they were not sure of the actual pin point location of the Grove, they were able to tell me it was part of a path leading to Bargedie a few miles along the Canal and the whole area was now Motorway or housing estates. Now every time I travel along the spot in the car Margaret says "Ok you don't need to tell me; Your Grandfather lived and died here".

There are a lot of unsolved mysteries on Grandfathers close family, one being, the fact that his brother Robert was a witness on his death certificate in 1927 yet Robert is on record as living and dying in Perth Australia in 1930. And by the way, Robert was married to a lass called Mary Elder Cowper. They were married in Bigger, Scotland and had a daughter called Agnes Swan Ewing

Well I am certainly not going to leave it at that. What about the women in his life? I am quite sure they were typical hard-working women of the day and I am sincerely grateful to the three of them.

His first marriage was to a lady called Jane Anderson Whitelaw who had stayed in the same street, she died at Crosshill Baillieston on 18$^{th}$ June 1897 and that's where cholera victims were buiried. They had had a very short marriage and no children? The death rate of women giving birth in those days was very high, local women being the mid-wives; I would not be surprised if this had been Jane's fate. After a few years mourning, on the 30th October 1903 he married Isabella Forsyth.

She was born in 1878 and would have been 25 years old when she became my Grandmother, Isabella had three children; George, Samuel (my father) and my Aunt Lalla. George emigrated to Canada and had a daughter called Georgina who I met only once. Aunt Agnes (Lalla) married a McGonagle and lived in Baillieston all her life, she had two daughters and one son. Grand-mothers father was George Forsyth born in Carmunnock in 1851 and her mother was Marion MacDonald born 1854.

A point of interest for some reason, probably seeing off friends or relations; prior to her marriage Grandma Isabella was in Liverpool 1901.

She died on the 14$^{th}$ of March 1914 from bronchitis with melancholia having lived at Rhindmuir road Easterhouse.

His third wife was Susan Brown I do not know much about Susan she had one child to George, a daughter called Rachel. Aunt Rachel married a Gent called Paten they had two daughters; one of whom married a Lord. I met her and her Lord once; she was a right beauty; took it from the Ewing's.

Aunt Lalla, was actually born Agnes, I remember her well, a wonderful lady. Here's a statement which sized her to a "T".

*An old lady climbed onto a bus and sat beside me. She opened her handbag and took out a rather squashed chocolate. "Here Son" she said beaming all over her face "I always gee a Sweetie tae the first stranger I speak tae in the day".*

Thank-you George Swan Ewing and Isabella Forsyth Ewing.

## Chapter 11

## Family Tradition.

Dailly, a strange name for a place, I wonder how it came about; no doubt Gaelic origin. Once part of a thriving community its main source of employment being the Kilgrammie Colliery where my great grandfather Samuel Ewing born 1842 spent his childhood. The ruins of the colliery are now one of the areas tourist attractions. Dailly is now unfortunately a pass through un-noticed insignificant little village in South Ayrshire.

Agnes Swan born 1842 married Samuel on the 8$^{th}$ March 1861. They had nine children, namely Mathew (1861), Samuel (?), Janet (1865), Grandfather George Swan Ewing (1867), Robert (1868), Mary (1869), Agnes (1872), Annie (1877), Maggie (1879). I can imagine Agnes Swan Ewing with that lot plus when they got older; all their kids over for Christmas, the mind boggles.

There were no washing machines or spin-driers in those days. No electricity or hot water on tap, it was scrubbing board in the take your turn wash house with the coal fired tub. Yes; and most of these guys worked in the Pit so there would have been a lot of washing. How lucky we are in this generation; can you imagine what their life was like? they had to share an outside toilet with other families and they were probably just as large. What an existence? My God we owe our ancestors so much, they were slaves to the upper class treated abominably even the children were put down the Pit, their schooling being how to push a wagon of coal.

Samuel and Agnes's families had been close neighbours prior to their wedding, in fact there were other marriages between the families. Agnes Lang Ewing born 1850 married George Swan on 19$^{th}$ Aug; 1870 at Kilwinning.

A point of romantic interest which probably had the wash-houses vibrating with gossip. Great Grandparents Samuel and Agnes as I said were married on the 8$^{th}$ March 1861 and their first child Mathew was born 4 months later on the 3$^{rd}$ June 1861. Tut-Tut-Tut.

No shame in that, I fancy they were lovey-doves. Having known one another since childhood and of course being a Ewing; Samuel had done the gentlemanly thing and made an honest woman of Agnes.

My God, Great Granny Agnes must have been some woman, nine children; her last at the ripe age of 40yrs. A fantastic achievement, to have brought up such a large family when poverty, disease and danger was rampant. What a wonderful devoted couple they must have been.

During their lifetime they fair travelled about, coal-mines didn't last long in those days. It was a case of dig a hole get the easy got at coal out, then move on.

Information from each of the children's birth certificates tells us where they were at that time.

Great Grandfather Samuel was born in Dailly then moved 50mls to Holytown where he started in the Pit at ten years of age. First son Mathew was born 1861 in Kilwinning 20mls from Holytown. both he and Agnes were 20yrs old and lived with his father Mathew. His namesake Samuel was their second child, not too sure when he was born. Then there was Janet born 1865, George my Grandfather born in 50mls away in Shotts 1867, Robert 1868 born in Lesmahagow 15 mls from Shotts, Mary 1869 born Kilwinning 50 mls, Agnes 1872, Annie 1877 born in Bothwell and Maggie 1879 in Dalziel15mls, a grand total of nine children; that must be a record number of cygnets from a Swan (think about it).

G Grandfather Samuel like his father had had no option but to follow the industry. Coalminers in those days went where the mine owners told them or starve. Samuel seemed to cover a helluva lot of coal-mines for some reason?

When I look at these dates and places and having been there, I realise how difficult it must have been to travel. How would it have been? horseback, coach, maybe by train. Anyway, one date and place stick's out, the year Annie was born in Bothwell 1877.

A day when two hundred and seven men and boys went from their homes as usual not knowing they would never ever see their loved ones again. The incident was the Blantyre Pit Disaster; probably caused by the intentional igniting of gas which was in those days the method of getting rid of it.

There was an explosion so severe that the blast shook the ground and created a gale force wind which smashed in windows and felled chimneys from roofs of miner's rows a mile up the road in Bothwell where my Great Grandparents and family lived.

The event is commemorated to this day on the site of the memorial.

Great Grandfather Samuel had been a coalminer all his life and died from Chronic Bronchitis, which was probably the dreaded and very slow death Silicosis, the infamous disease caused by breathing in coal dust.

I spent a lot of time searching for his and Agnes's burial place; no joy.

To reiterate, my Great Grandfather, Samuel Ewing (1841-1900) was married to Agnes Swan on 8$^{th}$ March 1861 in Kilwinning Church of Scotland by the then Minister Andrew Anderson. They both died in the Baillieston area, Agnes actually outliving Samuel by 27 years, she lived to the ripe old age of 86yrs' and would have witnessed the birth of her grandchildren one of them being my father Samuel. She was also alive to see her son marry three women; she would probably have done her Midwife for many of her Grandchildren including my father.

Thank You Samuel and Agnes

## Chapter 12

## A Brick Wall.

What a time to live, we can probably see an example in the present-day slums of Africa and these conditions continued for over a hundred years. Families had to survive on a pittance knowing the smallest words of complaint could mean being evicted and dying in the gutter on the street.

My 2x Great Grandfather Mathew Ewing was born 1807 in Ireland and at the age of 5 years moved to a village called Muirkirk in Ayrshire Scotland. Today there are only signs of the place once being a thriving community and it is sad that with such history it is now so insignificant. It has a fantastic history and had connections with the Robert the Bruce and William Wallace, (Their famous victories against the English were fought only a few miles to the north at Loudounhill). The Covenanters, Robert Burns and many famous Industrial entrepreneurs were also involved in the area.

Muirkirk will always be remembered for its 200 years and more contribution to coal-mining, there being a small looked after memorial situated in the centre of the village.

Mathew married Mary Davidson who was born 1810 in Muirkirk on the 8th July 1831. They had five children; Anne 1838, Samuel 1841(Great Grandfather), Mathew 1842, Margaret Newbury 1844 and Agnes Lang 1850.

OK that's all the easy stuff and probably 1800 will be where the majority of family hunters trail will end. Now things get really difficult, let me explain; Prior to 1830 British births and deaths were not certificated and the means of discovery was through church records or grave head stones. In fact, Mathew's death certificate was the last family related document I obtained.

It was for this reason for a year or two I was against the proverbial brick-wall, all the information I was getting although interesting seemed to be irrelevant with regards my family quest. Perseverance though finally wone the day as I will explain after a point of unbelievable interest

A few years ago, I was contacted by a lad called James Thomson from Glasgow who informed me we had the same 2x Great Grandfather and he was also against a brick wall. We communicated with one another comparing information and one of the most interesting things he told me to my mind was incredible.

This you couldn't have made up; in fact, it would make a terrific script for a lovey-dovey movie. I'll explain it the best I can.

My 2xGreat Grandfather Mathew's daughter Margaret Newbury Ewing married James Thomson on the 18$^{th}$ September 1862. They were present day James Thomson's ancestors.

Also, 2x Great Grandfather Mathew's son Mathew married an Elizabeth Brown and they were present day Annie Robertson's ancestors.

Now what odds would you give for descendants of brother and sister Mathew and Margaret to meet over 100yrs later and after getting married discover they had the same 2x Great Grandfather. I would give a million to one easy.

James Thomson and Annie Robertson from Glasgow, one in a trillion couple they should be in the Guinness Book of Records. What drew them together; was it love at first sight; a reunion with hereditary influence; did they see a family resemblance in one another. I just cannot believe it was a simple coincidence, this to my mind was similar to my coal-dust in the blood syndrome. Easily a million to one chance, makes one wonder.

Here I go again, no I'm not going to consider the Supernatural, I'm certainly open to suggestions though. Two people not knowing they were kin, meeting one another as complete strangers and in later years discovering they had the same 2xGreat Grandfather, there are millions of people in Glasgow and they picked one another. Unbelievable.

Anyway, that's something I had to mention I thought it truly remarkable. Maybe out of context but as I've said on numerous occasions -It's the way I tell em-.

Now; this is where you the reader will have to bear-with me and really give it a bit of thought. I will do my best to explain how I discovered who my ancestors were in Ireland. I appreciate there are those who will not accept my assumptions; they being the Lawyer hardliners who will only accept legal documentation.

Believe me I mean no disrespect and I am open to comment.

All QPR and Census records for the early 1800's in Scotland were for births, marriages and deaths. Unfortunately, in Ireland records of births were few and far between and my only resource initially was his death and marriage certificates. So of course, I had a bit of detective work ahead and I realised it would be no easy feat to break down that brick wall.

My 2x Great Grandfather Mathew was born in Ireland and he was only a baby when he came over to Scotland.

His death certificate stated he was born in Ireland in 1808, was a coalminer and died in Kilwinning Ayrshire in 1870 and had married a Mary Davidson. His father was Samuel (a soldier) and his mother was Emilia Blaney (more likely Blayney).

I spent so much time hunting through so much information and I was getting nowhere. All that effort and getting no results. It would have been the sensible thing to admit I was as I said earlier up against the proverbial brick wall and give up. I just couldn't; I was trapped, like my "coal in the veins syndrome" I now had the "genealogy in the blood syndrome" It was all I could think about.

I needed a bit of inspiration; a bit of luck and it came from my friend Tammy in Canada. We had been in e-mail contact for a few years and she was also on the hunt for her Irish ancestors. What she discovered and I give her all the credit was hard to believe and it actually took me some time to appreciate its significance. In fact, I almost put it in the bin and when it hit me, I was lying in bed at the time, I was simply overwhelmed.

When I explained my assumptions to Tammy and other acquaintances, I don't think they agreed with me? It certainly took a bit of Sherlock Holmes delving into and I am not even sure that I eventually convinced them.

It was a genealogist's dream of a find, a handwritten document compiled by a lady called Enola Ewing in 1930 and brought up to date by her sister Anna Ewing Ranns who brought it to light in 1991. I got my break-through, at last I had knocked down my brick wall and I was on the heavenly cloud nine.

I cannot say enough to praise this writing, remembering that this was researched not from the computerised world we live in today but from discussions with elderly family members, writings in bibles and visits to graveyards. The time and effort which must have been put into it in itself proves a character worthy of the Ewing name; Enola Ewing and Anna Ewing Ranns I congratulate and thank you very much.

The most relevant part of the document states that members of her family moved from Ireland to Muirkirk in 1812.

Rather than show the whole of it I will quote parts and explain their relevance to my own assumptions. Unfortunately, only part one is available, (Copy of the document can be viewed at http://ripandrevmedia.ca/files/ )

I quote

Mathew Ewing (Snr;) married Ann Kelly.

They had at least three sons and a daughter. The eldest son was killed in the war under Wellington who defeated the French at the battle of Salamanca in Spain in 1812. The youngest son settled in the USA and his son fought in the Civil War. The daughter married a Mr Lang. The middle son James Ewing born 1785 died 1876. He ran away from home in County Tyrone Ireland and went to Scotland during the Bonaparte Wars. James and his wife Jane Percy came from Scotland to Pike River, Quebec Canada in 1822 with their three children.

Family hunters must appreciate how lucky I was to obtain this document, only hand written scribbles which confirmed all my own previous findings. It was in fact the missing piece of the jig-saw I was searching for. An unbelievable piece of fortune which is self-explainable and easy to compare. Let me explain;

I found James and his wife Jane on Register IGI for Ayrshire having christened daughters Anne 18th July 1819 and Margaret 12 March 1816 in Muirkirk.

The document stated James moved to Muirkirk during the Napoleonic wars.

Also confirmed on the Ayrshire QPR for marriages, an Anne Ewing had married a John Lang on the 28$^{th}$ Sept 1823 in Muirkirk, a very interesting point here is the fact that my gg Grandfather Mathew named one of his children Agnes Lang Ewing. As stated on the document the daughter married a Mr Lang.

The youngest son must have been Robert who I later discovered had registered the Christening of his daughter Anne on 31$^{st}$ Mar 1822 on the Ayrshire IGI for Muikirk. Robert's son Joseph distinguished himself by fighting through the whole of the American Civil War.

Having established the identities of three of Mathew and Anne's sibling's and proving the relationship between them and my established family I must believe categorically that the eldest son who was killed at the Battle of Salamanca was Samuel Ewing my 3x Great Grandfather.

It was also stated on the document that Mathew Ewing (Snr) and Ann Kelly were their parents which makes them my 4x Great Grandparents.

When James and Jane moved from Ireland to Muirkirk, they were also caring for four-year-old orphan gg Grandfather Mathew. This wasn't stated on Enola Ewing's document but I am pretty sure this was the case due to my findings which I will show later.

With the obvious absence of Mathew Jr; Parents and Grandparents, the significant mother figure looking after all his needs would have been 22-year-old Aunt Ann. A bit of reasoning backing this up is when Mathew had children of his own, he named his daughters Ann and Agnes Lang Ewing, Lang being his Aunt Ann's married name.

It was very common in those days for families to pass on similar Christian names. In fact, when comparing family trees of descendants of Mathew and Ann Kelly the names Samuel, Mathew and Ann are very prominent.

In 1812, Mathew would have been 4 years old, his uncles Robert 12 and James 25. His Aunt Ann would have been 22 years old.

Thank you, Enola Ewing, for giving me the path of discovery to my Scots Irish ancestors.

What has to be appreciated now is that I am personally convinced that my 3x Great Grandparents were Samuel Ewing and Emilia Blaney. Also, I am 100% positive my 4x Great Grandparents were Mathew and Anne Kelly.

My goal now is to attempt to find further ancestors in Ireland. Unfortunately, as I said earlier Genealogy prior to 1820 is just that little bit more difficult, nowhere more so than in Ireland; no informative Census's or *Birth/Death Certificates; and of course, due to the troubles a lot of records were* destroyed. Yes, a lot of detective work was now required, things weren't going to be easy.

Before we go any further let's have a little respite, relax, have a dram and let me take you on another car journey. We will take the same route I took my American friends Dick and Karen. By the way I was really embarrassed on that occasion when I got lost, I had taken the wrong cut-off on the M74 and almost ended up 20 miles north of my destination. A little blether with a local farmer a few laughs and we got on the right road again.

I'll not get lost this time we'll use the sat-nav.

Just a few miles from my home in Muirhead we get onto the M73 and pass where I was born, Gartcosh. Then, only again a few miles on the motor-way the place where my father was born and his father died. Bailleston, in fact the area is where my family have lived over the past 150 years. Not far from there it's onto the M74 the major motorway to Carlisle and the country of the auld enemy, England.

We don't go that far though, it's through Bothwell, Hamilton then the Motherwell area where I worked in the gigantic Ravenscraig Steel-Works for over 20yrs. Another ten miles on the M74 where we cut of onto the A70, its then another ten miles along the desolate country road where we reach our main destination.

It's a now a little inconspicuous village where my Irish ancestors were initiated into Scottish industrial life, a place called Muirkirk, we almost missed it. It was raining and miserable amidst the moor and hills. A few cottages in the middle of nowhere, with plenty ruins in the middle of muddy and desolate fields.

There is a small museum and a quaint little coffee shop.

We walked about a bit and discovered a small memorial to the coal-miners who had worked in the Muirkirk Pits. Appropriately there was a statuette of an eagle next to the memorial. Our next find was a nice little grassy area called the 'Covenanting Heritage Lay-Bye'. I couldn't believe it; there; in the centre of this park, a plaque commemorating the setting up of the first ironworks in Ayrshire by James Ewing & Co in 1787. My American cousins were as astonished as I was.

Here it was ; Proof that the Ewing's were a major power in Muirkirk. This gives credence to the Ranns document where she states Muirkirk is our ancestral home. What a discovery; there must have been Ewing's in the area prior to my lot arriving from Ireland; which explains them travelling so far.

My assumption has to be the James Ewing on the Plaque was related and had rescued the Ewing's from the troubles in Ireland

Now why would anyone wish to destroy this fantastic natural scenery. Unscrupulous, hard-hearted and greedy individuals; who earned their wealth from slavery that's who and unfortunately the Ewing's (not my lot from Ireland) had a major part in carrying it out. Muirkirk turned out to be one of the initial areas to be involved in the start of the Industrial Revolution in Scotland and to this day shows the aftermath - an industrial poisoned wasteland.

Having established Muirkirk was Ewing's starting off point in Scotland. Let's ponder and talk a little about the place, after all Mathew spent his childhood and teenage years there and I'll try to say something nice about it.

It's a wee village I didn't even know existed even although I had passed through dozens of times. Sits in the middle of Ayrshire Scotland and has quite a history. It was Covenanter country, and which goes along with a few of my theories. One being my ancestral home was Muirkirk.

During the middle of the 17$^{th}$ Century the Covenanters rebelled against King Charles II and after many battles which were referred to as "Killing Time", a final battle defeated the Covenanters at Bothwell Bridge. I believe the Ewing's were

Presbyterian Covenanters and had to flee from the wrath of the King to Ireland.

A hundred years before the battle of Bothwell Bridge it is recorded that Mary Queen of Scots while retreating from the aftermath of the Battle of Langside resided in Muirkirk.

A lot of archaeological work has also been done in the area and prehistoric sites along with Bronze Age graves were found proving life existed in the area thousands of years ago. I wonder; who can say; is Muirkirk where my roots are?

Muirkirk once one of the largest industrial sites in Britain, as I said now a little village with a fantastic history where sadly very few stop to view.

I will be referring to Muirkirk on a few occasions throughout my story, in the meantime let's get on the road again About 10mls along the A70 and we arrive in Cumnock, Ayrshire, this is where my 2x Great Grandfather's uncle Robert, (Dick Childs direct ancestor) married in 1820, the church is no longer there. There is a quaint little museum on the site where the staff are very helpful although parking can be difficult.

This part of Ayrshire was very much so, a coal-mining area, Pits all over the place. One in particular called Knockshinoch had a disaster in 1950 which became an international media event. More than one hundred miners were trapped for over three days, thirteen died.

"The Brave Don't Cry" is a terrific film giving a great account of the event and like my own story "WHY" gives an accurate description of the hardships coal-miners and their families had to endure.

According to records there are many Ewing's who lived in Ayrshire and probably there were many of them coal-miners. Although I can find no record of any involved in this particular disaster, I am quite sure they were there or thereabouts and point of interest there are 17 Ewing's living in Russia.

It's only a few miles and we are in Alloway, birthplace of Rabbie Burns then into the towns of Ayr and Prestwick. They are really one big town and I love the place. The walk along the beach is wonderful and the Carlton hotel in Prestwick serves a lovely fish and chips.

Heading for home we arrive in Kilwinning home of that infamous Lord Eglington and where Mary my ggGrand Mother died 1860 from Cancer; she is buried in "The Churchyard Kilwinning". Mathew also died in Kilwinning in 1871 I assume he is also in the Churchyard.

I had previously spent a day in Kilwinning just walking the streets and thinking about Mathew and Mary, I searched for the Church Graveyard; no joy, there were a few churches no longer in business. I searched for a Ewing on the Gravestones in the Abbey, no joy. I left a flower on the site as gratitude to my great great Grandmother Mary.

Mathew and Mary certainly moved about during their lifetime. Muirkirk to Daily (married $8^{th}$ July 1831) then Auchinleck back to Dailly then Newarthill in Bothwell and ending up in Kilwinning. There is no doubt both Mary and Mathew my gg grandparents had a horrible and distressing time during their suffering latter years. One having had the Cancer and the other the slow dying terrible Coalminers Lung (Silicosis).

Thank You Mathew and Mary. My Great Great Grandparents.

Ok let me summarise

William Ewing (1941-?)
Samuel Ewing (1909-1969)
George Swan Ewing (1867-1927)
Samuel Ewing (1842-1900)
Mathew Ewing (1807-1870)

# PART THREE
## IRELAND

## Chapter 13.

## An Irish Orphan.

What a revelation? discovering my 2xgreat Grandfather was Irish was a complete shock and having to take joking abuse from my niece's husband was a bit much. I was certainly put back about it, the people I knew with Irish blood were all Celtic supporters. Would this change my allegiance towards the famous blue nose Glasgow Rangers? of course not; There's not a team like the Glasgow Rangers no not one. (first line of supporter's song).

Of course, do not think for one moment that I am bias? I have a lot of friends who are of Irish descent and this little piece of information; -that I have a bit of Irish blood in me- brings me closer to them. It also had me delving into Irish history and what I dug up was mind-boggling, the atrocities carried out on the Scottish by the English were bad enough, the ones done to the Irish people were even worse. The English throughout the 17$^{th}$ and 18$^{th}$ Century were responsible for the deaths of millions of Irelands people, both Protestants and Catholics. Their objective being to rid the country of Irish and install English and their Allies, this system of events was referred to as "The Plantation"

What a crowd of monsters, evil in the extreme. The Irish had got the same treatment the Scots had got before and after the Battle of Culloden. Whole villages along with their occupants vanished, completely obliterated, women and children slaughtered, no quarter given. Famines were created by polluting or burning crops, murder and whatever was taking place on a massive scale. One of the English infamous entertainments was to barricade the screaming terrified people into their local church and set it on fire.

1812 as I have stated was when my Ewing line came out of Ireland, I reckon they had been there for those previous 200 terrible years. Did they take part in those terrible atrocities? Were they in league with the English? They certainly were gifted Irish land during the 17th Century Plantation and fought for the English on several occasions. I'm not going to go any further on the subject, just let me say; Even thinking about it makes me feel ashamed and it brings a tear to my eyes.

I believe the group which included my ggGrandfather who came over to Muirkirk in 1812 had all lost their parents. This being the case, they had probably been evicted from their land. The only kinsmen they had was James Ewing who was the owner of the famous Iron-works in Muirkirk Scotland.

What a terrible place Ireland must have been when the Ewing's were there, and it didn't get any better after they left. The real big and devastating famine of them all happened in 1845. It is reckoned over one million people died in what was called the potato famine. Some say the famine was orchestrated by the English, I find this hard to believe, although when you think about it? A bit of a coincidence when it was going along with what the English were attempting to achieve.

I feel I am treading on dangerous ground? Let me change the subject and give you a bit more about my family.

Samuel Ewing ( -1812) and Emilia Blaney were my 3x Great Grandparents. They came from Tyrone Ireland and had one son my 2x Great Grandfather Mathew.

I had discovered this from Mathew's death certificate and Anna Ewing Ranns document. the first stated that his father Samuel's occupation was soldier and the latter that he was killed at the Battle of Salamanca.

Samuel no doubt was a soldier in an Irish Regiment involved in keeping the peace in Ireland and when the armies of Wellington became desperate for men they decided to recruit in Ireland. Having had spent considerable effort recruiting in Scotland with little success, the 74th Highland of Foot Regiment had to have a go in Ireland in 1809. Yes, they were desperate, they had lost so many men in previous battles they even decided to drop their honourable tradition of only recruiting Scots.

I do not believe for one minute that the Irish would be clamouring to join up, there was probably some sort of enforced conscription on the go. More likely the Press-gang method where many a poor lad woke to the sound of the bugle not knowing how he had got there and how he had got the big bump on his head.

The Regiment sailed from Cork in 1810 and joined the 1$^{st}$ Brigade in Portugal under Major Gen Picton: Which in turn later became part of the third Division.

Two hundred years after the death of my 3xgreat Grandfather Samuel, Margaret and I decided to give Cork a visit. The city has been a major port for hundreds of years and was a main setting off point for emigrants to far-off shores. Many of my kin left this port for a new life in the USA. Even this far South I discovered a James Ewing born 1754 and a John Ewing were from Cork.

After all these years of course, the place has totally changed, the city is literally a nightmare of shopping malls and crowds of shoving and pushing women. One conciliation; it has a pleasant walk along the banks of the River Lee.

The dock where Samuel and his Regiment had set off is no longer there but I'm the fantasist I can use my imagination.

I see it as it was: the sailing ships tied to the Docks and the soldiers being marched on board. I see the cannon and ammunition; the cavalry horses being led onto the gangplank. I visualise my one-year old 2xGrandfather Mathew being held in his Aunts arms and being hugged by his crying mother and father before they venture on board. In my minds-eye imagination I see it all. Sobbing women holding their babies and watching the ships leave the harbour, the soldiers waving their goodbyes from the deck. A very sad situation and I had to take a deep breath to control my emotions.

My fantasise ended with a jolt as we came across a relevant image, a memorial to those who left Cork for far off shores. An appropriate statue of a mother and her two children looking out to sea as if they were seeing off a loved one. I have to admit when I saw it, I shed a few tears. My thoughts were of my 3xGreat Grandparents on that ship not being able to take their eyes off Ireland until it was no longer in sight.

Samuel and Emelia must have experienced some horrific adventures in Europe. Napoleon; we've all heard of him; another little Hitler who wanted to rule the world, and if he had not been so greedy, he probably would have.

He and Lord Wellington were having great fun, having battles, killing thousands and grandstanding with the ladies while it happened.

I carried out a lot of research regarding Samuel and Emelia's time in Europe, I appreciate it may be of little interest to the majority who are not related so I will approach for the moment my findings on my family line and stay in Ireland.

Do not concern yourself, I intend devoting a full chapter on them later.

OK According to Enola's document Samuels family came from County Tyrone. I had names, time and County. I wanted a more precise locality so I hunted.

I found the Christian names very common all over Ireland but eventually my persistence paid off. There in Donaghmore, Co Tyrone, Northern Ireland on the Flax Growers Bounty List for 1796 were my Ewing's.

They were Flax growers and Weavers. So, I would reckon having their own business they would have had some standing in the community. Of course, they would still have been under the jurisdiction of the hierarchy. When his Lordship came along with the fiery cross they had to follow.

How long my Ewing's had resided in Donaghmore I did not know, I do know that Ewing's were given land during the 17th Century during the time of the Plantation. To understand what I am talking about you must be knowledgeable on the history of the period. I'm not going to go into great detail, just let me say as I have said before the English ravaged the country and handed it out to his faithful Lords, Eglington being one of them. My thoughts at this time were that my distant ancestors were part of the Plantation having had a connection to Lord Eglington during the 19th Century.

I spent considerable time trying to locate the whereabouts of the six Ewing's I had discovered in Donaghmore after 1796. Nothing other of course than James who went to Muirkirk and Samuel who was killed at Salamanca. What happened to the other four I do not know? We must assume either along with my 3x Great Grandfather Samuel they went to war and perished as did so many of their countrymen.

Donaghmore, a right lilt to it Irish name, don't you think? It sits there on its lonesome next to the River Torrent on the outskirts of the town of Dungannon not far from the border with the Republic. A beautiful countryside unscathed by human hands. So much so there must have been a very traumatic reason for my Ewing's to leave.

Emelia Blaney my 3xgreat Grandmother, I scoured many records looking for information about her, all to no avail. I'll bet she was a lady, dressing in all the fineries, going to the Regiments balls and keeping company with the aristocracy. I find it a beautiful and uncommon name, Emelia; it's got a touch of class,

The name itself gives me the impression she was a bit of a toff, unfortunately her life-style would have been short and sweet. She had a very short marriage, the war in Europe bringing it to a catastrophic end. Oh, I hope she initially had some happy times, I'm sure she was a beautiful and caring woman. Maybe the birth of her son gave her some happiness, rest in peace Emelia.

One very interesting find though was that the name Blaney had the honour of having the County of Castleblaney named after it and her namesakes had been peers of the realm. In fact, a John Blayney (Blaney) was among the officers who swore to defend the city of Londonderry in 1689 and fought for King William, it's also a name prominent in Co Monaghan and is today mainly in Counties Antrim and Down.

Margaret and I visited Monaghan and Castleblaney in 2014.

Another terrific place to visit in Ireland is the Blarney Castle which is close to Cork and a must is the kissing of the Blarney Stone. I done the kissing, while lying on my back and supported by a hefty Irishman. It was supposed to endow me with "the gift of the gab". No way-I'm still a quiet don't bother anyone respectable guy.

I reckon Samuel was a young man when he died in 1812 and not long married to Emilia Blaney. I wonder what he was like, was he like me, did he appreciate the wonders of nature, was he fond of life, scared of dying; God it must have been a terrifying experience, I have been so fortunate in my lifetime never to have faced a war, my time in the army was mostly spent marching and saluting. Nowadays we have an option, conscription in Britain ceased in 1959 young people are no longer under duress to take up arms.

The nearest I ever got to fighting was while on exercise we were attacked by a parachute regiment and they charged at us with bayonets fixed. We all got drunk after it, if the exercise had been for real there would have been a lot of washing to do next day that's for sure.

## 14. Chapter

## Eagle Wing

It was 1760 when my 4x Great Grandfather Mathew was born and he lived all his life in Ireland. History tells us of the poor living conditions at that time, I wonder, could he read and write, was he one of the under-privileged poor. I don't think so? I believe he would have been a very intelligent entrepreneur who had been wealthy enough to finance his son Samuel into the army as a Lieutenant. In those days it was money not experience or talent that decided who ruled in the British army and similar to civilian life there was class distinction between officers and men.

As it is today and will probably never change, there was a disgraceful difference between the living standards of the wealthy and the poor. The wealthy were building their fancy big houses while the poor were living in wooden or muck walled and floored sheds, if they were lucky.

Anyway, I feel I am being a bit nasty and harsh on my ancestors, what options would they have had. If they were one of the wealthy land-owners which I believe they were, what could they have done to help the poor.

We'll change the subject; I have previously mentioned my wanting to work in the Coal-Mines since I was a child. That terrific magnetism that I had been born with due to my ancestors being miners for the past 200yrs. Yes, I believe I was born to be a coalminer, it was my roots and I would have been one all my working life if my wife hadn't persuaded me to move to the Steel-works.

You will probably be saying it was a coincidence; no? I believe there are certain things passed down from father to son. As I said the attraction for working in the Pits was in my blood. I also believe my ancestors having lived in Ireland left me with a strong affection for the country. Even before I knew about my family connections I desperately wanted to visit. On the 24th September 1962, we got married and our Honeymoon destination; guess what? of all the places we could have gone, I picked Ireland and believe me at that time I had no idea my ancestors had lived in the place for 200 years.

Got the cattle-boat from Glasgow to Belfast, didn't sleep much our cabin was close to the engine. A lot of lovely memories, it was our first experience being involved with the Irish people, they are in my opinion the most sociable and friendly individuals you are likely to meet.

Our first encounter was really an example of the Irishman's attitude to life. We had got off the boat and on finding a taxi rank with plenty cars, could not get a driver. A passer-by informed us they were in the Pub. It was early morning and they were having a drink; "OK" I was informed "I will be out shortly" We had to wait until he finished his pint of beer. Guess what our destination the railway station was about 100yds away, we could have walked it no bother.

The train journey was another laugh a minute, it was that slow you could have picked the daises as it rocked from side to side.

Can we call it coincidence, maybe? I do not think so. This was another case of -It's in the blood-. Of all the places in Britain and I picked Bangor in

Ireland, the country of fairies and pixies, it makes the hairs on the back of my neck stand.

And just walking distance away from Bangor there's a town called Groomsport, significantly the birthplace of that famous ship "The Eagle Wing".

Here I was not knowing how important that ship had been to the Ewing family, they had chartered or maybe even built it themselves over 300yrs ago and emigrated to America. I believe it was no coincidence Margaret and I spending our honeymoon in Bangor and finding the Eagle Wing. The experience stuck in my mind and wasn't I surprised many years later when I discovered genealogy and the Eagle Wing connections.

Like my coal dust in the blood syndrome, Ireland had the same magnetism. I just loved the place, unfortunately just after our visit life became horrendously unbearable on their streets. Cowardly attacks were taking place against the innocents, bombs going off in crowded areas, women and children being blown to pieces.

The beautiful land with their beautiful people was at that time -Hell on Earth- and a no-go for tourists.

It wasn't until 1995 when we again took the opportunity not only for a second honeymoon; but also, to walk the footsteps of my forefathers; we toured Northern Ireland. Forgetting the concrete blocks around police stations, the experience was absolutely fantastic.

We explored the whole coastline of the North from Bangor to Londonderry even into the Republic to Inch Island Donegal and Letterkenny, areas where history states Ewing's were prominent.

I have been in many countries throughout my life and in my opinion, there is no other that can beat Ireland for friendliness, we both loved it and it won't be long till were back again.

Yes, I have Irish blood in me and I am proud of it, there are no nicer people on this planet. My 4xgreatGrandfather was Mathew Ewing Snr born 1760 in Ireland, married Ann Kelly, born in Ireland. They had three sons and one daughter. My 3xgreatGrandfather Samuel, born in Ireland 1787 who married Emilia Blaney born in Ireland, James born Ireland 1789, Robert Ewing, born Ireland 1800 and Ann Ewing, born 1791 in Ireland.

I know I have mentioned Enola and Ann Ewing Rann's's document previously and I will refer to it probably on a lot more occasions. (Copy of the document can be viewed at http://ripandrevmedia.ca/files/ ) I don't care, I will intentionally mention it over and over.

It is a terrific scribbled down piece of information and deserves bucket loads of praise. Ann Ewing Ranns ancestor was James Ewing who was the brother of my ggg Grandfather Samuel.

## Chapter 15

## Not an Act of God.

Still in the 18$^{th}$ Century in fact to be exact 1740, Britain was hit by severe cold weather. Ireland was cut off from Britain due to Ports being blocked by ice. That whole year in Ireland was unbearable, it got hit by inconceivable destructive weather, whether it be drought, gales floods or snow and it accompanied a terrible famine. The aftermath of it all was breakouts of smallpox, dysentery and typhus. There were riots, hunger marches and murder on the streets. Law and order were non-existent, people were starving and desperate, the only hospital in Dublin was overflowing and unable to cope. The population was dying and there was no help being given from the ruling body. Out of a total population of 2,500,000 there were 450,000 deaths.

At this time across the pond to America would have been a good idea and my 5x Great Grandfather James Ewing born 1725 with his wife Ealoner Auld did just that. He took with him his children Samuel, Alexander, Henry, John, Moses, James and Jean.

He came from Donegal and died in 1785 in Chester Pennsylvania, for some reason his son Mathew my 4x Great Grandfather born 1760 stayed behind in Ireland.

There you have it; again, my ancestors were off to America. I reckon they went between 1760 and 1780. God Almighty; that ocean must have been a busy place? all those little sailing ships like the

Eagle Wing going back and forth carrying people who were looking and expecting a better existence.

What a shock they must have experienced; this was a terrible killing time in America, there was a war going on where thousands were being killed. One historical battle was at Bunker Hill, over 1000 British troops died. The Americans were fighting for independence and winning. The crucial point is; Was my 5xGreat Grandfather a soldier? Part of the British army fighting for the English. The unthinkable part of this theory is that there were probably, in fact definitely already Ewing's in America fighting for the Americans.

A General James Ewing is on record as fighting on the side of America under the orders of a Commander Montgomery at the battle of Quebec in 1775. Could this General be my 5x great Grandfather. I believe it is possible? There were actually thousands of Ulstermen fighting for the Americans and the Montgomery's were associated with the Ewing's in Scotland and Ireland.

You might think me inappropriate by jumping back and forth through the centuries, it's just my style. I try and make things interesting for everyone so let's diverse a little and let me tell you again about one of our experiences in my favourite country Ireland.

After an all-day sight-seeing in the wonderful city of two names; Londonderry (the South call it Derry) we of course got a bit peckish (needed to eat). I was all for one of the plentiful Pubs but Margaret preferred somewhere quiet. Now this was difficult; after at least an hour of hunting for a restaurant we found one hiding itself up a side street. A nice comfortable and quiet little place with a reasonable menu. After a considerable wait we got service and gave our order and the girls reply in a lovely Irish twang without an apology: "You will have to wait the Chef is watching a football match".

I love visiting Ireland, their lay-back attitude to life is absolutely fantastic. It is a great pity that there are elements of hatred between their peoples.

## Chapter 16.

## America.

To have survived in Ireland during the 18th Century was an achievement, that's for sure. My previous chapter tells it all. The famine was devastating, 400,000 people died and the resulting formation of resistance groups who took their revenge on the wealthy including the Protestant Landlords made life a hell on earth.

It is no surprise that my Ancestors decided to take the enormous decision to move to America. My 6x Great Grandfather was I believe the main man who made the final decision, Henry Ewing born 1701 in Ireland took with him his wife Jane Allen, his son John and his grand-children (see previous chapter) he died 1782 in Chester County, Pennsylvania. Five brothers and a sister were already in America so no doubt the trip was to end as a family reunion.

It is not surprising so many Ewing's moved to America, Ireland was a shaken wasp's nest during the 18$^{th}$ century, the poor peasants were rebelling, their conditions were appalling and they were easy pickings for individuals wishing to create their own little rebel armies.

What am I talking about? The whole world at this time was a terrible mess, there were wars continually over every continent. Americans were killing one another while giving the British a right doin during their Revolution which by the way resulted in the Independent United States. The French also had a tussle resulting in the Monarchy losing their heads to Robespierre's guillotine. The seven year's war during the middle of the 18$^{th}$ century was also a topper involving most of the European countries. There is no doubt this time was a killing time. Human trafficking, slave trading was at its peak, working men, women and children were treated like cattle; bought and sold at the market.

This is appalling, what am I creating here? a horror story? So far, I've killed millions. I'm supposed to be entertaining; I love this Country. Ireland and its people as I know them, they are absolutely beautiful. I would even go as far to say if there was somewhere on this earth that I would like to live other than Scotland it would be Ireland. Yes, I've been to Florida, the Canaries, Canada, Spain Portugal, Germany and many more. Scotland and Ireland top the lot. By the way Germany would be bottom of my pick.

I suppose the 18$^{th}$ century had its good points, maybe few and far between, there was James Watt's steam engine, a Scotsman from Greenock. The first air flight took place; It was a hot-air balloon with a duck, a chicken and a sheep on board. Which brings to mind another of our experiences; let me cheer you up a bit, have a giggle.

It was in a typical little Irish middle of no-where country village. There was a goat tied to the fence, it's owner probably inside having a pint. The dilapidated building was actually a hotel although the residential part was closed. There was nowhere else for miles where we could have got a refreshment (a wee dram) so after a bit of pleading I convinced Margaret to join me.

The place was unbelievable and would have been closed if we had been health and safety inspectors. Persuading Margaret to stay was mainly due to my desperation for a pint of Guinness. The décor of the room was something to behold; wallpaper had been torn from areas behind the large burst armchairs and tacked over beer-stains on the wall. In fact, some of the patches were upside down. The Hotel's cliental were typical Irish farmers, everyone shouting across the room at one another: Each with their own topic of conversation. The farmers were dressed in their working clothes and still had their shitty wellies on, which were comfortably resting on the tables. The highlight of the night which superseded any hotel entertainment I have ever experienced was when the barman received a phone-call and we overhead him saying. "OK Paddy; bring him in" He then proceeded to lay newspapers on the bar. By this time, I was enjoying the company, contemplating another pint and intrigued by the reason for the newspapers.

The door of the Lounge was kicked, someone wanting in. I being the gentleman that I am opened the door. A burly farmer carrying a full-grown sheep walked in. Margaret and I were in total shock and a bit hysterical. I thought I was going to have a convulsion; I could not stop laughing. The locals must have thought me mad; no doubt it was a regular thing for them; sheep at the bar.

It turned out that the barman was also the local veterinarian. How they got the cows in to that lounge we'll never know. When I asked the farmer if the sheep was his date and we got the evil eye look; we thought it safer to do a runner. Not to America; just a few miles along the road to our Bed and Breakfast accommodation.

Yes, the $18^{th}$ Century was one helluva time and the world was a horrible place. But where America was different was; it had unexplored territory ready to be inhabited and migration was encouraged and accepted. It was a growing fast country and it was being filled with not only Scots/Irish but people from all over the world.

My goodness; this was also the time of the sailing ship, there must have been hundreds of them coming into the American shores. I wonder how the American Indian felt? The poor guy must have stood back and wondered at it all. Of course, he eventually realised what was happening and like the Jacobite's and the Irish peasant they were slaughtered while defending their land.

# Chapter 17

## Aristocracy.

A Baron, usually addressed as "your Lordship" is a position of nobility, a title which is hereditary and ordained by the reigning monarch. They were the wig wearing gentry, very wealthy, extremely powerful and important individuals. The judge and jury live or die decision makers of their day. Do not underestimate this gentleman, he would have had his own private army of servants, soldiers and oppressed serfs to farm his land and do his bidding. He could have called to arms hundreds of men and have them die for his gratification. He would have had high authority in Scotland England and Ireland making decisions which would have had effect on the whole country.

Baron William Ewing, born 1660 in Stirling would have been such a man, a knight, an honour bestowed on one of his ancestors and passed on to him. He, was my 7xGreat Grandfather and I am not proud of the fact.

I was a bit surprised to discover his Lordship on my family line, I was under the impression my ancestors had been wealthy entrepreneurs, merchants or high-ranking soldiers. The fact that my 3xgreat Grandfather Samuel in 1812 had been a Lieutenant in the army made me think his father would have also been a soldier. Of course, to have been an officer in those days one had to be a gentleman of wealth and there is, no doubt descendants of the Baron who came into that category.

Discovering the Baron answered another of my queries; My DNA results told me I was kin to the Orr Ewing's who are to this day Lords and Ladies of the aristocracy, his lordship is probably where our heredity connection lies.

I am maybe being a bit of a socialist, remember I was a coal-miner, it's just that I believe the Aristocracy during this period were totally evil. They believed the common man was vermin and treated him accordingly. How could a man have his tournaments entertaining, live in luxury and feed his friends on the best while children living in his domain were starving to the extent, they were cannibalistic.

Enough of that for the moment, I do get carried away and believe it or not I am talking about my ancestor.

As was procedure the title of Baron was passed down from his father who had brought him and his siblings to Ireland from Scotland, which king endowed the honour and why he left Scotland is a point of conjecture. I would tend to think he was sent over to strengthen the Protestant held strongholds or maybe to escape the wrath of Oliver Cromwell who had defeated the Scots and taken over Stirling Castle in 1650.

The Barons children were, Henry, John 1695-1751, Joshua b1697, Capt. James 1703-1800, Samuel 1705-1758, Anne, b1706, William 1710-1782

You will notice that all the Barons children with the exception of Henry have birth and death dates. This is due to the fact that they were taken from American sources. With the exception of Henry, they all died in America and as I stated in a previous chapter Henry was my 6x Great Grandfather.

I appreciate that there will be those who will question my findings, information prior to 1800 in most cases is regarded as conjectural and open to scrutiny. I have certainly done my best to ensure that everything is correct and above board.

Please contact me if any discrepancies are found, just remember I have kissed the Blarney Stone and enjoy a bit of an argument.

My goodness things are getting a bit complicated, I hope you are still with me. Do not be confused over the next chapter, the main-man, he was also a Baron in fact the father of Baron of the same name William.

## Chapter 18

## The Main Man.

This was the culprit; this is the one who was responsible for bringing my kin to Ireland. What the Hell made him do it? He was a Baron for God's sake. He was living the life of royalty, a castle full of servants, he could have had anything he wanted. Why did he leave it all and take his family to the Hell on Earth at that time; Ireland.?

Baron William James Ewing born 1625 in Stirling Scotland, married to Elizabeth Ewing was my 8x Great Grandfather.

The Ewing's were Covenanter Presbyterians and Masons, hated by the then Catholic rulers. The Catholics got the upper hand during the mid-1600s and enjoyed a bit of cut and thrust slaughtering so the Ewing's hightailed it to Coleraine in Ireland.

There was also the possibility that the Baron was getting away from Oliver Cromwell's forces who had invaded Scotland and won battles at Dunbar, Preston and Stirling eventually capturing Stirling Castle in 1651.

Cromwell gave no quarter and murdered thousands during this campaign in Scotland.

The Baron must have felt himself a lucky guy, what with all that killing taking place he managed to high-tail it to what he thought was safety.

Little did he know? Cromwell's forces were similarly executing thousands in Ireland at the time. Oliver was another do as your told or get the sword little Hitler and the Baron no doubt had to follow orders in order to survive.

There is also the possibility he had an army with him and was taking part in the onslaught against the Irish people.

He and his family had lived during terrible times in both Scotland and Ireland. Let's assume though, he having been persecuted, seeing family and friends executed and homes destroyed were having to flee for their lives. It would be a horrible thought to have had him engaged in the terrible atrocities that were taking place in Ireland at this time.

The Baron would not have been long in Ireland before he would have had to perform his fighting skills; The Catholic forces had a large army and were on the rampage killing and destroying everything in their path. It was 1689 and the Rebels had the upper hand the Protestant forces being under siege in their last vestige, the city of Londonderry.

I will not go into the specifics just let me say; The fighting lasted for 105 days, 30,000 defenders refusing to surrender, there was a fierce bombardment and great loss of life.

There were many Ewing's who participated in the defence of Londonderry. Proof being the fact that the Barons son John in on record as being a Burgess in the town and after the 1690 Battle of the Boyne when the Protestant King William of Orange won, John emigrated in 1728 to Chester City, PA. He had been married twice and keeping up with tradition had nine children.

The Barons children were John, Captain Charles Findley, Robert, James, William, Henry, Patrick, Anne, Elizabeth, Margaret and Francis.

Another bit of proof the Ewing's were involved in the Siege.

In Hampton's "Siege and History of Londonderry, 1861", p361, is the statement.

"The first meeting of the Corporation of Londonderry after the exclusion of the Irish from the city was held 2$^{nd}$ January 1689/90 Present, John Campsie, Mayor, -, Alderman, John McKinney. Chamberlain-Sheriff. John Ewing, Burgess."

In Douglas's *Darrian*, or Hampton's *Siege of Londonderry* is this old poem, "Londeriadoes," section five of which has the following lines:
I love it.

> James Roe Cunningham and Master Brooks
> Gave great supplied, as are seen by their books
> Ewin and Wilson, merchants, gave the game
> And forty merchants, which I cannot name
> Horace Kennedy went into Scotland
> And moved the Council some relief to send.

It is said that six Ewing brothers fought at the Boyne and two were killed. I dispute this I reckon The Baron along with his seven sons were there.

Captain Charles Findlay was awarded a silver sword by King William in recognition of his bravery during the battle. I have death dates for all which do not correspond with being killed at the Boyne except Patrick, Alexander and Robert. I therefore conclude that it is feasible that the latter three were killed.

The Baron who died Feb 18th 1717 in Ireland. was also knighted by King William

As per usual, the battle had been all about royalty bickering about who was going to rule the roost.

The Catholic King James11 determined to exterminate the Protestants, press-ganged an army of peasant farmers to fight alongside his Jacobite and French patriots. He had believed the Protestants would have surrendered the City of Londonderry but he was mistaken.

Prince William of Orange came to the rescue, with his 36,000 men he routed the army of James killing over 1,500 of his men.

Here's part of an old poem written shortly after that battle by a native of Ireland.:

Hindman fired on Antrim's men
When they with wild Maguire
Took flight and off thro' Dermott's glen
Thought proper to retire
Dalton, Baker's right-hand man
With Evans, mills and Ewing
And Bacon of Magilligan
The foe was off pursuing.

Appropriate, don't you think, 'Ewing' rhyming with 'pursuing'; this gives definite confirmation they were involved.

# PART 4

## Chapter 19

## Scots-Irish

Donegal County, Ireland. One of the most delightful places in the world. Margaret and I spent some adventurous time exploring

Let me enlighten you a little.

Ballymastocker Bay has the second most beautiful beach in the world according to the Observer Magazine. A must if you enjoy a paddle, although be warned the North Atlantic can be pretty cold no matter what time of the year. Better sticking to dry land, since seeing the film Jaws, I haven't put a toe in the sea.

Then there's Malin Head the most northerly point of the whole of Ireland, if you like a bit of seclusion, then this is the place, and the views from the top of the cliffs are fantastic, even Scotland's coastline can be seen on good days

Inch Island, many of my readers I am sure will be aware of this little bit of lands significance, although only a few miles from Londonderry city it is a very secluded and isolated part of Donegal where Ewing's have resided for a few hundred years.

Of course, we cannot forget our supernatural friends from the other side. Donegal castle is a spooky place situated in the city of Donegal and is reputed to be the most haunted in Ireland if not the world. Many sightings of strange movements of mist which forms into apparitions of human and animal like creatures have been reported. During our visit we identified no ghosts, although one resident we did discover had been a Lord Montgomery Eglinton from the South West of Scotland. No doubt doing the English's bidding.

Everyone likes to visit ancient sites, whether it be Roman forts, ruined Castles and even the old stuff like Stonehenge. Well this is the place it has the lot, for instance there is a massive ring fort where it is said one of the earliest kings Eogan MacNeill 465AD lived and died.

Ireland today is divided into two, the North which is part of Britain and the South which is an independent country. Donegal is quite a large County and today lies in the South and typical of Irish humour the northern most point of Ireland is in the South.

William James Ewing who was born in Stirling 1605 and died 1665 in Donegal Ireland, married to Ester Ewing was my 9x Great Grandfather.

On the other side of Ireland on the Antrim coast close to Larne there is Ballygally Castle. The reason I'm mentioning this is because it is rated as one of the top ten most haunted sites in the world and was refuge for Protestants during the 1641 Irish Rebellion. The ghost is apparently a wife who was locked in the tower because she could not bear a son. She in trying to escape fell from the window and was killed. There are many hair-raising reports of seeing and hearing her wandering around during the night. The castle is now a hotel and for the believer a must to stay the night; her name was Isabella and the room is a showpiece.

This was the time of "The Plantation" where the English were handing out Irish land to their friends and alias. The Ewing's; my ancestors being accessory to this is pretty disturbing to say the least. I would have preferred them to have been common five eight coalminers. I stated in chapter eighteen that his son the Baron was the main man I was maybe wrong, it was probably a joint venture and they were rewarded well, landing high ranking positions of grandeur in the army and civilian life.

This was a revelation for me, I knew my ancestors came over to Muirkirk, Scotland from Ireland in 1812. What I had wanted to know was; were they of Scottish or Irish origin.

I had believed initially that they had been ruled by Lord Eglington and moved from Ayrshire to Ireland to work his Plantation plot. I never thought for one moment that they were aristocracy from Stirling and of similar status as his Lordship.

Anyway, this changed things, the Ewing's from Stirling were certainly of high status and held positions of authority in Scotland and thereafter Ireland. My ancestors helped the English of that there is no doubt and I hate to say it; they were rewarded for doing so.

There you are now, how many friends have I lost? My last few paragraphs have probably lost me my membership of the Ewing Clan. As if things weren't bad enough; Last night I attended an EGM at my Golf Club and it was announced the Mount Ellen Golf Club which I have been a member for almost 40years has been put into liquidation. That's equivalent to at least 200 friends lost. I know your heart bleeds for me? just thought I'd change the subject for a moment, it was a travesty, Mount Ellen only 12 years ago had the reputation of being the friendliest and best kept golf-course in Lanarkshire with assets worth millions of pounds today suspiciously it has nothing and is even leaving debt.

I wonder if any of my ancestors played at golf? Don't laugh, the game goes back a bit and I believe like other things it's in my genes.

After that little bit of useless information let's get back to reality and sanity?

William James Ewing my 9x Great Grandfather did not have things easy in Ireland. The Irish were not taking the intrusion into their country without retaliation. As I said earlier with the help of the Catholic Church and French, they organised a rebellion. It resulted in thousands of deaths on both sides and created bigotry which remains to this day between not the Irish and English but unfortunately between Catholic and Protestant. The Irish and Scots had been friends and allies for hundreds of years, here they were split right down the middle. This was caused by the initiation of religious bigotry and this happened in 1641. It changed Ireland forever.

## Chapter 20

## Stirling Castle.

Now this is the castle to beat them all, one of Scotland's best, not a ruin, a perfect building. It sits majestically on a natural high plateau giving astounding scenery from its parapets, the hills and glens to the north on a clear day are absolutely beautiful.

Before the age of cannon, it must have been unconquerable and to think, Ewing's took part in both defending and attacking its walls. I can just imagine them looking down at an advancing army and preparing themselves for battle, to see in the distance all those fighting men with their assault towers and large sling-shots. What an experience it must have been? They were very brave men; that's for sure, they would have known that there would have been no quarter given, it was fight to the death.

The castle is certainly a fantastic monument for the history of Scotland and stands supreme. There are no soldiers required nowadays for its defence although that famous infantry regiment the Argyll and Sutherland Highlanders have it as their headquarters and their museum displays many of their battle trophies and certainly worth a visit.

My wife Margaret and I have visited Stirling on many occasions and been in the castle quite often and I had never thought for one moment that my ancestors had actually been residents. All my discoveries so far certainly point to the fact that they were and it is a bit a nonsense to believe that in

1812 my 2xGreat Grandfather having had a father with such a noble background turned out to be a poor serf of a coalminer to Lord Eglinton in Ayrshire.

William Caldwell Ewing born 1580 in Stirling, was married to both Janet and Eliza, not at the same time I presume and died 1665 in Scotland he was my 10x Great Grandfather. He died the same year as his son, this was one hell of a time, it was when the country was hit with the horrible "Great Bubonic Plague" referred to as "The Black Death". I hope they died a normal death; the Plague was definitely not the way to go.

William would have been witness to Oliver Cromwell's siege on Stirling Castle in 1651, marks on the walls from cannon and musket ball still exist. It was obvious that the artillery would not have taken long to destroy the Castle. Subsequently it was surrendered to Cromwell without bloodshed. The Scottish forces then became allies with Cromwell against the Royalists.

Cannon was the weapon of the day and was getting more advanced each year. The Mons Meg now on display in Edinburgh castle will testify to that. There is no wall in the world could stand up to its devasting force.

God these Ewing's: trouble seems to follow them, they sure had plenty of it throughout the generations.

I personally have often been regarded as a trouble maker. If it's the case that I am then it is obvious where it has come from.

You know? I have read so much bumph and hobby-cock about Ireland and Scotland's history my head is thumping. There have been so many battles, so many different factions involved, Protestant, Catholic, Williamites, Papists, Cromwell's

Parlitarians, French, Jacobite's, Covenanters, English, Scottish, Royalists, Fenians and probably a lot more I've missed. What this all achieved was bitterness and hatred in the extreme for centuries and most of them were royal family squabbles.

This man, William Caldwell Ewing my 10x great Grandfather was born and died in Scotland so he would legally be Scottish. I do not know to what country his allegiance lay? I have my suspicions.

## Chapter 21

## A Reverend in the Family.

What a discovery? I just do not believe it, an Ewing a preacher, a man of the cloth. This must be a mistake? and he's family; simply unbelievable. I have often joked with my grandsons that we should have a minister in the family saying it was up to them and there we have it.

Reverend William Ewing born 1565 in Scotland; his son William Caldwell Ewing was born in 1580 and according to my calculations he started young. He married Helen and had a son when he was 15yrs of age.

The Reverend was my 11xGreat Grandfather and he died 1640 in Londonderry Ireland.

Here is more proof I am from Scottish blood, why though did he move from Scotland to Ireland. This was one Hell on Earth of a time to live in Ireland, chivalry had gone out the windae. Scorched earth along with kill everyone including women and children was the policy of the day from both sides. Of course, the clergy were a different entity in those days, not like today where the congregation consists of a few sitting in the front pews. The church had their own armies and were very powerful with their own laws. A non-attender as was a girl who misbehaved were severely dealt with. One scene from the film -How Green Was My Valley- comes to mind where a woman is degraded and disgraced by the minister in front of a packed church for having a child out of wed-lock. You'd better believe it, the church was powerful and the clergy were just as cruel as their masters, living a life of luxury comparable with the hierarchy who gave them their orders and paid their wages.

William lived for 75 years, that in itself tells me he had led a privileged existence, there is no doubt he managed to look after himself. No venturing out into the villages rife with disease for him. His life would have been alongside the high-class peers with the Londonderry walls and cannon to keep him safe.

Life expectancy for the commoner during William's time was with a bit of luck forty years.

Between 1580 and 1605 in Ireland due to the deliberate destruction of crops by both sides, there were terrible outbreaks of famine. It was so bad that cannibalism was rife, in fact people were removing bodies from graves for sustenance. One horrible instance was where five children were found to have eaten their mother.

The Reverend was probably a Protestant Presbyterian minister, quite a position in those days unlike today, I'll bet his church would have been packed. I would like to think he acted as a minister of God and helped those starving people.

Depending on who was in power and what religion they were decided the fate of individuals. If the Reverend was Covenanter, he would have been lucky to avoid losing his head. He would have been a constant target, if captured by the Catholics he would have had to endure extreme torture and a violent burning at the stake death.

Atrocities were being committed by both sides during the 16th and 17th centuries and really came to the fore during the Irish rebellion and when Oliver Cromwell decided to have a retaliatory real go. He killed thousands of the population, including Catholics, Protestants, women and children.

His actions are regarded by historians as being the main reason there is hatred between Protestant and Catholic in Ireland to this day.

I wonder what Reverend William said to his congregation, was it a case of forgive and turn the other cheek. More likely kill or be killed, what a terrible time, it wasn't a case of one battle let's go home. This was perpetual killing and it all started mainly because of a royal family feud. Why couldn't they have just left the people to live a peaceful life.

His life span covered a very historical time, Henry viii the English king who had six wives and beheaded two of them. He crowned himself king of Ireland and was of course responsible for most of the terrible atrocities which took place at that time. Our own king James vi became the first to become King of Great Britain and of course the "Scottish Reformation"; It was during the $16^{th}$ century that Scotland became a Protestant country and this was probably the reason Rev William went to Ireland, to spread the word

## Chapter 22

## Flag-Bearer.

All these years 500 in fact, and so far, no mariners, I'm disappointed, these were the years of the "Sea Dog" privateers. Sir Francis Drake was doing his pirate thing for Queen Elizabeth and of course helped in repulsing the Spanish armada. Surely, we had a buccaneer out there? Some gallant cutlass swishing hero cutting down those Spanish rascals. No record I'm afraid, there was money to be made in sailing back and forth to America though and a little on the big money-making slave-trade.

There is no doubt a branch of the Ewing's made a lot of money and I mean a lot of money from the slave trade, having owned both ships and colonies in Jamaica. Fortunately, I have found no connection to any of these distasteful and horrible ventures with my direct line ancestors.

Middle of the 16$^{th}$ Century a time when religion was having a lot of fun, HenryVIII started the band wagon rolling by denouncing the Roman Catholic Church and creating a religion to suit himself. Then when Kinky Henry died a new queen brought England back to Catholicism, resulting in bloodbaths where hundreds if not thousands of protestants were burned at the stake or hanged.

England certainly had their religious troubles and Scotland was just as bad, Mary Queen of Scots a catholic had that old fox John Knox to contend with and he had a lot of supporters, so much so his principles eventually won the day and Scotland took on the Presbyterian Protestant religion.

All these shenanigans as usual created more and more battles, the poor peasants coming off the worst. Thousands being killed in wars created by Protestant against Catholic and even to this day religion still being the reason for conflict.

My 12x Great Grandfather William Ewing lived during all this turmoil and I believe he probably had a part in it. His time was 1535-1600 born in Scotland and married to Catherine.

In fact, I believe William had a very big part in it, my assumption is he was a part of the aristocracy of the time and carried the flag for Mary Queen of Scots at the battle of Langside in 1568. A point of interest is that the Lord Eglington also fought for the queen and after her defeat not only changed his religion to protestant but changed his allegiance to the English king. Eglington was lord and master over most of the South West of Scotland and had a lot of say in who received land in Ireland (The Plantation).

If William did fight for Mary, it is possible that he was actually Catholic at the time. Scotland was predominately Roman Catholic prior to the Reformation which commenced around about 1550. In fact, most of Scotland as I said changed their allegiance to Protestant, Presbyterian during the mid-16$^{th}$ century.

I also believe William was one of Lord Eglington's Knights and he and his family would have changed their religion to Protestant then were designated land in Ireland.

Well this is certainly a bit of conjecture, but think about it? These were people with a bit of standing, aristocracy, why would they pack up and move to Ireland. There must have been one big reason. They weren't run of the mill peasants these were landowners cashing in from all their tenants. Leaving Scotland was forced on them. It certainly looks like my Kinsmen done the sensible thing and hightailed it off to the Emerald Isle to avoid the big chop?

# Chapter 23

# A Gathering

What I am going to write for you in this chapter is not fiction. I'm taking you back for a moment to my generation. It was a once in a lifetime experience; One I would never have believed could have taken place. All the years I have been working on my family tree and discovering so many cousins yet never meeting them. This was my opportunity and I wasn't going to miss it.

Wednesday 28$^{th}$ August 2019.

This is our third day in Dunoon, so far, the weather has been kind. The fresh salty air and sunshine has put a little colour into our cheeks. The Esplanade Hotel sits right on the shore with our window looking majestically over the sea to Ayrshire and out onto the Atlantic, just beautiful.

Let's not forget though? The big main reason for my visit is for the Ewing Family Association (EFA) and Clan Ewing gathering plus of course the Cowal Games. I have been an honouree member of the EFA for the last 20yrs. And a member of Clan Ewing since its inauguration five years ago.

This is the first time the 99% American group have had their annual gathering in Scotland and the first time I have been able to attend the event. I am certainly looking forward to meeting fellow genealogists who have been on the Ewing trail like myself for many years. The experience should be interesting.

Margaret and I had already met most of the EFA committee when five years ago in Glasgow we were guests at the inauguration of the Clan Ewing. That was a wonderful and gratifying experience and they must be congratulated on the outcome.

On this occasion they have organised a large group of approximately 40 Ewing's from America to not only attend the Cowal Games but also amongst a short visit ternary they will visit the McEwan Castle and other historical sites. Believe me these are exceptional people and even though we had different views and friendly arguments over the years on their website I look on them as family.

How many of us can claim to have met in person for the first time, 45 cousins whose relationship began over 300 years ago? Well this 78-year-old has had that honour this lovely morning. I just could not believe my eyes; our meeting place was the Hunters Quay Holiday Park. The hall was packed with men and women wearing identification cards around their necks, everywhere you looked there was an Ewing.

During my lifetime in Scotland I reckon I have other than my own family only met one other Ewing. He was a fellow engineer in the Ravenscraig Steelworks and here I was meeting a hall full of cousins.

Immediately I felt like the star of the show? It looked like Margaret and I were the only Scots and the Americans were quick to respond to my offer of introduction. It was like a scene from the televisions "Long lost families", I was overwhelmed, it was absolutely amazing, all these individuals were descendants of my Irish forefathers. We were related and we had discovered one another over many years with the help of that wonderful world of Google.

Beth Toscos was the perfect organiser a typical Regimental Sergeant Major Ewing, everyone was put on parade and given their position in the convoy of vehicles. Unfortunately, there were four souls left without transport so myself being the proper gentleman offered to take two in our small Hyundi, they were a very nice couple from Virginia, Mike and Brenda Ewing. Actually, I had been hoping selfishly that the group would have had mini-bus's available for the trip to Kilfinan. Reason being; I was looking forward to company; maybe a sing-song and I had to change my car due to damage caused on the same bad roads when we travelled on them a year previously.

I took no risks this time; so it was the long road to Strachur then down to Tighnabruaich and back up to Kilfinan. Certainly, a long road but safe and my passengers appreciated the scenery, especially from the viewpoint overlooking the Isle of Bute which is one of the best in Scotland? The Hotel was comfortable but like most they ripped us off by charging £13.50 for a plate of watery soup, two small sandwiches and a cup of coffee.

Decision time? Will we accompany the Americans across the fields, ditches and swamps? No chance; once bitten twice shy as they say, I led them the first mile or so gave directions then returned to the nice dry lounge, yes, the rain came on. They were off in search of the McEwan castle, a very muddy and wet long two miles. We waited for them approximately 3 hours then it was back to Dunoon safe and sound.

Thursday 29$^{th}$ August.

Again, we were meeting all our American cousins. This time in the Dunoon Burgh Hall not far from our hotel. The weather wasn't too good and Margaret was recovering from a broken Hip so a Cab was in order.

After an introduction from Beth Ewing Toscos, Thor Ewing gave a lecture on the Clan Ewing; a lot of information but no definite proof of our origins. I was impressed but disappointed, I had hoped for even a little tit-bit of data which would have proved categorically that our roots were from Scotland, sadly it didn't happen. After Thor came David Ewing who gave us information on our DNA project, again impressive but nothing to convince me our roots were Scottish.

Oh, please before I join my ancestors; someone belay my fears and give me proof that my origins are Scottish and not English.

During the taking of photographs the officials very nicely invited me into their group which I found very gratifying. In fact, it brought a tear to my eye.

We said our goodbyes I will probably never see them again.

Would you believe it while back at the Hotel sitting in the Lounge having a refreshment a young perplexed lady came in. There is no doubt she was worried and Margaret whether she had seen a resemblance or whatever asked if she was an Ewing.

Yes; she was; Catherine, a school teacher from Maine USA, her sister Hope had lost her luggage during her flight. They had just arrived after 35 hours travelling and been told at reception that their room had not yet been paid for. We done our best to console them for a while, then to rub salt into the wound they were refused a table for dinner. What a start and they were scheduled to walk the West Highland Way the following week.

Friday 30$^{th}$ August.

The Cowal Games are in progress and Clan Ewing have a stand/tent at the Stadium. As the locals say it is Cowal Games Weather, there is a 60mph gale along with perpetual rain and a flood warning in the area. As we are not prepared for the elements and old enough to realise the stupidity of being soaked, we will forget the Games and stay in the Hotel for the day.

Saturday 31st August.

What a night; the rain belted down and the wind blew, it was horrendous we hardly got a wink of sleep. It was still raining when we came back from breakfast and were dead beat. The decision was made; pack up and go home.

## Chapter 24

## Anti-Climax

OK let's get back to history; Sorry, not a happy ending I'm afraid; this is as weird as it can get, the ghosts are all coming out and laughing at us, the past is giving me a complete sense of failure and despondency. In fact, I feel I should maybe for the moment give up and leave it for someone else to figure it all out.

You the reader must be thinking I am an old fart. There hasn't been a good word from me for the Ewing's since we hit Ireland. I suppose they were living life as it was laid out for them and they had no option. In fact, they probably done the most honourable thing by hijacking it off to the America's.

My final discovery hit me like a ton of bricks, something I have suspected and feared since I came upon the Baronies and my DNA connections to the Orr Ewing's. The idea that my ancestors had been involved with the goings on in Ireland was hard enough to take but this was ten times worse. Like salt being put onto the wound it brought tears to my eyes.

My 13x Great Grandfather James Ewing was an Englishman.

Here we have it, James Ewing my 13x Great Grandfather, born 1500 in ENGLAND married Katherine Ewing, he died 1560 in Scotland.

How is this possible? the English were at war with Scotland for most of his lifetime and I assume he like his descendants were resident in Stirling castle. In fact, there was one big major battle during his lifetime which the English won at Musselborough, Edinburgh in 1547. It was the battle of Pinkie where thousands of Scots were killed.

He was probably an Aristocrat or a knight who fought at the battle of Pinkie for his country.

Where's the justice? All this bloody work and I end up with an English forefather. I suppose it's been on the cards right enough; mediocre common five-eight individuals do not become Barons or are knighted by their sovereign and presented with silver swords. There were so many Ewing's in positions of authority during medieval times in towns and castles spread out over Scotland and to have had the honour of being the Queen's flag-bearer. I find it inconceivable that James Ewing's ancestors were from a Scottish Clan.

Right through to the present-day modern times there were Ewing's regarded as being amongst the richest people in Britain. They built replica castles all over Scotland, took part in financing projects throughout the industrial revolution and have their name on the official list of peers of Henry vii who reigned over England 1485-1509.

This was the icing on the cake, or more like the last-straw, Henry vii was totally through and through an English king a Tudor no less and I do not need to dig too deep into history to discover he was responsible for many deaths just to keep himself in luxury on the throne.

Five hundred years, that's a helluva lot of water under the bridge. How many descendants can James Ewing be attributed to, remembering they were a randy lot. I would reckon that he has the majority of

Irish American Ewing's on his family tree. In fact, James has been responsible for at least tens of thousands of descendants the majority living in the USA.

I am going to continue searching for my English ancestors even if it means travelling into the land of the "Auld Enemy" it will not be easy but will make a terrific sequel and I might even give it out free. Sorry I'm a Ewing haven't made my first million yet, maybe charge a fiver.

I started on my family history all those years ago with so many unanswered questions and I am ending it with many more. I am sorry I am just tired and anyway why should I give you a happy ending. I fear for what the Ewing's were further back in time.

What can I conclude from all this gobble-gook, I really hate to say it? How can we say these people descended from rag-tag clansmen from the banks of Loch Fyne? My heart and soul want it to be so. They say truth hurts, my God if what I fear is true, say no more.

What did I tell you earlier, I could create an argument in an empty house, of course all my data is conjectural and debateable? I hope in my lifetime someone will come up with proper proof that the Ewing's are true Scots.

You know what? I feel like banging my head against a brick wall, the sensations I am feeling right now, an aspirin would not be sufficient.

My head is nipping, surely the Ewing's are of Scots origin? Prove me wrong, please. Everything points to James Ewing coming from England, I have searched and searched for any Ewing in Scotland before 1500 Not a sausage, everything points to my suspicions. The Ewing's have English blood. Yes,

I'll give it a bit of welly and give that wall the Glasga-kiss (bang my head on the wall) I'll no sleep to-night and when my coal-mining ancestors discover all this they will turn in their graves.

One consolation is the fact that James's sons were born in Scotland therefore all you American Ewing's can refer to yourselves as Scots Irish Americans. Anyway, what does it matter; as the Ranger Supporter says--We Are the People--.

PS one very marvellous invention was created around about the year 1500 which some will say would be handy for the disposing of this story.

The first flushing toilet was brought into use.

# PART FOUR
## AMERICAN AND CANADIAN COUSINS

## Chapter 25

## Emigration.

Thank you for not flushing my story? I hope we are still friends and you have got over the shock sufficiently to read on.

The Ewing's were amongst the earliest emigrants to arrive on the shores of America, they saw no future in both Scotland and Ireland. The countries were being torn apart by constant religious bigotry and hatred. This was their opportunity to start afresh, a new life without the daily fear of having to watch their backs and being drawn into wars of which they had no interest.

They took the plunge and decided to take on the adventure of a lifetime and what an adventure it turned out to be. They were amongst the earliest pioneers who had to start from scratch, living off the land, making their own laws in fact everything was there to be built on and the Ewing's were the ones who took advantage.

It is a fact that there were Ewing's among the first of the Pioneers who ventured into America long before my ancestral cousins from Ireland. I do not have proof of any connections but I'm sure they would have been kinsmen.

What I do have is that the sons of my ancestor Baron Ewing 1605-1665 chartered a ship and sailed to America. The Baron had 14 children. His son

Baron William James Ewing born 1625 in Stirling Scotland, married to Elizabeth (Eliza) Milford didn't do too bad himself having eleven. The Baron died Feb 18th 1717 in Ireland.

Children- John, Captain Charles Findley, Robert, James, William, Henry, Patrick, Anne, Elizabeth, Margaret and Francis.

I believe that most of these twenty-five with their own families (up to 10 children apiece) were passengers on the Eagle Wing ending up in Tennessee, Virginia, Maryland and many other states of America.

It is also possible when the captain saw the amount of Ewing's coming on board, his comment was "We are going to need a bigger boat".

During the 17$^{th}$ and 18$^{th}$ Centuries England used America as a dumping ground for the so called 'undesirables. They had a policy of transporting criminals and trouble makers to the Colonies; the souls were treated no better than slaves on their arrival.

In 1716 four ships left Liverpool with 300 Jacobite prisoners bound for the Colonies and after the defeat on Culloden Moor in 1746 many more followed.

People could also take passage on the understanding they would pay-back by working for their patron when they arrived.

Don't get me wrong Baron Ewing's lot paid for their own voyage, in fact they were wealthy enough to purchase land and were well educated.

Then there was my ancestor James Ewing born 1725 died 1785. He was married to Elinor Auld they came from Donegal Ireland. Was born in Ireland and died in Chester Pennsylvania USA. He had seven sons and one daughter. Samuel, Mathew, Alexander, Henry, John, Moses, James and Jean.

Mathew did not go to America the rest of the family probably did along with their father.

The Ewing's participated in helping not only to create one of the richest and greatest countries in the world, they also contributed in making America one of the highest populated.

It is estimated that there are 32,925 Ewing's living in America that's 10 times more than what's in the United Kingdom. (This estimate was given ten years ago, it's probably doubled, maybe even trebled by now). My God, are they all the Barons descendants? I wouldn't be a bit surprised.

I used to think we could have held a reunion in the family department of my local Pub, looks like Hamden Park would be more appropriate.

I hope I am not confusing one, my direct blood line did not go to America. I'm a Scotsman, my ancestor was one of the few who chose to go back to Scotland. By the way my Scottish lot had big families to.

There is no doubt the Barons children and their descendants made a name for themselves in America and their stories would have been best-sellers. JR Ewing comes to mind, that was a terrific show. Do we have an Ewing cousin in the oil game as rich as JR? if so, I'd like to meet him, maybe have a blether over a game of golf.

Sorry I'm getting carried away with myself, let's get back to the nitty-gritty.

The Baron and his family had been wealthy and managed to pay their passage to America. I don't really know whether the Ewing's who went over in the 19th and 20th centuries were so lucky. Maybe paid for by American cousins or as I suspect they were indentured, which meant they had had their passage paid for them by a patron to whom they were indebted to when they arrived in America. Not a very nice situation to be in when it is appreciated, they could be in the hands of unscrupulous slave owning landowners.

There was James Ewing 1785-1876 my 3x Great Grandfathers brother who had accompanied my 3yr old ggGrandfather Mathew when they moved from Ireland to Scotland. He emigrated from Muirkirk along with his wife Jane Percy to Pike River, Quebec, Canada in 1826.

They had Anna 1819-1908. Francis 1826-1879, Mary 1827-1845, Elizabeth 1832-1866, Martha 1834-1936 and John 1821-1914. A young family at the time of their voyage, in fact was Francis born on board?

James only had one son to carry on the Ewing name, the lad certainly lived up to tradition, John had 7 boys and 2 girls.

This was still the time of Sailing ships, the majority of which were adapted for the purpose of transporting slaves. Indentured passengers were accommodated no differently, their cramped and communal bunks had to be endured for at least six weeks if the wind was in their favour.

James traditionally had a lot of descendants, some of whom I had the pleasure of communicating with. They like myself are infected with that wonderful engrossing world of Genealogy. You know; when you think about it, it's a good job the Ewing's scattered, I doubt very much the present-day Scotland would have been large enough to hold them all.

I wonder? these guys that went off to America are they the ones or related to the ones that are mentioned so much in history. Anyway, I'm raving on a bit again let's change it for a bit.

I have always enjoyed a good movie; preferably historical ones. "The Patriot" starring Mel Gibson is brilliant, he plays the part of a leader of Militia fighting the British 1775-1783.

It is definitely a true-to-earth film and doesn't beat about the bush in describing atrocities from both sides although it was a little; step back in amazement bias towards the Americans.

The hand-to-hand fighting sequences are out of this world, terrific and of course you will also appreciate that I am going to tell you that Ewing's were involved in the war.

Col; Thomas Ewing was such a man. During the Seven Years War he commanded a battalion of Maryland militia against the British, there was no quarter given; ambush 'hit and run' tactics were the order of the day. There are many stories of his exploits, one in particular suggests he was pretty close to the President.

From a historical document we learn:

"President Hancock sent a verbal message via Col. Thomas Ewing, commander of a battalion of Maryland militia with the flying camp, requisitioning militia from four Maryland counties to assist in Philadelphia's defence."

Also, on record in Col; Thomas Ewing's Battalion for the Flying Camp, July 26$^{th}$ 1776, there was a Virginian, George Ewing (1754-1824), who also fought against the British.

Col. Thomas Ewing became a prominent business man. So much so he was later United States Secretary of the Interior (1849-1850), three of his sons were Union Generals in the civil war and notably General Sherman, most famously known for his Civil War 'March to the Sea' which devastated a wide swath of land leading from the captured city of

Atlanta, Georgia, to the port of Savannah, was married to Thomas Ewing's daughter Ellen.

And I'll bet if we could get a DNA sample, we would find that Thomas was a distant cousin.

Here's a bit of interesting information

ILLINOIS. William Lee Davidson Ewing (1795-1846), Senator and acting Governor (1834), was of Ulster Scot descent.

"The Eleventh Earl of Eglinton from Kilwinning in Ayrshire led the 78th Regiment of Highlanders for the British in the American campaign during the Seven Years War (1756-1763) and was commended for his expedition against the Cherokees." I thought the British lost that war? I'll bet our brave Earl didn't even see a Cherokee?

There was a Virginian George Ewing (1744-1824) who fought in the same war against the British.

## Chapter 26

## Robert Ewing

If anyone throughout my research deserves credit it's this man. One whom the descendants of 2x great Grandfather Mathew owe a great debt to. His name Robert Ewing 1800-1869.

Mathew was a 4yr old orphan when Robert was 12, he was Mathew's uncle. There is no doubt Robert was responsible for Mathew's safety and saved his life on many occasions.

They both worked together in the Pits of Ayrshire for over thirty years and were very close.

I could write many chapters about the coal-mines in their day, in fact I have a book published with Amazon Kindle about coal-mining. It's called Why, worth a read. https://www.amazon.co.uk/Why-Colliers-Tale-William-Ewing-ebook/dp/B07FZMZKWM

I'm not going to give you a speel about how it must have been for them working underground, just let me tell you they were risking their lives every-day in death-traps and anyone working in them needed someone to watch their back.

Robert was Mathews compatriot and brother of that there is no doubt.

The first indication of Robert and his family in Scotland is on the QPR for Muirkirk, Ayrshire, Scotland. Ref 607/3, Frame 811, and I quote.

"1820. Robert Ewing and Mary Williamson both belonging to this Parish were regularly proclaimed in this parish church in order to marriage and married at Cumnock on the 29th of November." (Muirkirk is only a few miles from Cumnock).

I had the pleasure of visiting Muirkirk and Cumnock along with Dick and Karen Childs. Dick is a descendant of Robert's, his mother being an Ewing.

They were both enthralled to see a plaque commemorating a Ewing who had actually owned the Ironworks complex and realising this was where their distant ancestor Robert had lived all those years ago.

Both villages are but a speck of what they were in Robert's day, Muirkirk still having the ruins of the Industrial site that blackened the area and Cumnock unfortunately having a new church built on the site where his wedding took place.

The births of their first four children were recorded in the Muirkirk QPR as follows:

QPR for Muirkirk, Ref 607/3, Frame 662

1822 Robert Ewing and Mary Williamson. Megslee a daughter born 24th March and baptised on the 31st named Anne.

QPR for Muirkirk, Ref 607/3, Frame 671

1824 Robert Ewing and Mary Williamson. Kirkgreen a son born 3rd April and baptised on the 6th named William.

QPR for Muirkirk, Ref 607/3, Frame 679

1826 Robert Ewing and Mary Williamson. Burnside a son born 23rd April and baptised 21st May named Mathew.

QPR for Muirkirk, Ref 607/3 Frame 691

1828. Robert Ewing and Mary Williamson Burnside a son born 9th September and baptised named Robert.

Weren't they consistent, every two years, anyway we'll not go into that?

They also moved about a bit, Megslee, Kirkgreen and Burnside being names given to Miners Rows in the area.

I wonder what life was like in those far off days, one thing for sure in Muirkirk where Ironworks, Coal-Pits, Tarmacadam's works and many other ancillary works prevailed, along with the cold and wet climate it would have been pretty miserable that's for sure.

You might wonder why I'm giving Robert precedence. Well it's because he was not only responsible for keeping my 2x great Grandfather safe he was also the key to me discovering Mathew's whereabouts in those early years.

That's 16yrs in Muirkirk and working underground, Robert and Mathew would have been fully-fledged coalminers after that amount of time. They then moved to Daily in the South of Ayrshire between 1828 and 1830. Probably instructed to move by the Mine-owners. Daily is approximately 40 miles from Muirkirk and only 5miles from the sea. I'll bet they saw a difference in the air quality. They maybe even got a paddle on the sea-shore at Girvan, that's if they got a day off.

There were two births recorded in the Dailly QPR for Robert.

Samuel 1830 Ref 585/2 and John 1835. Ref 585/2, Frame 534.

Again, this was coalmining territory. and famous for the tale about John Brown who was entombed for a considerable time before being dramatically rescued. (The story is in my previous book WHY).

Margaret and I spent some time exploring Dailly, wasn't enamoured I'm afraid. the place was very quiet, typical of what was an old one time mining village.

On the 1841 Census for Daily in the district of Kilgrammi there is listed a family called Ewens. I quote;

Robert Ewens 35 Coal Miner Ireland, Mary Ewens 35 Ireland, Ann Ewens 15,
Matthew Ewens 15 Coal M, Robert Ewens 12 Coal Miner.
Samuel Ewens 10 Coal M, Susan Ewens 5.
Wm Ewens 3, James Ewens.

Ann Williamson 70 Ind, Ireland (probably Mary Ewens mother).

It is noticeable that William who was born 1824 is not listed and a new son has been given his name, also added to the family are Susan and James.

The first William could have died anywhere between the age of three and 17years, was William killed as a young coalminer?

Also note he has named his sons Mathew and Samuel (as per my 3x and 2xgreat Grandfathers).

I hope this is not getting to be a bit boring, all these facts and figures, I know they give me a bit of a sore head at times. Let me finish Roberts time in Ayrshire by telling you about another of my adventures.

It was a few years ago when we took Margaret's brother and sister in-laws advice and visited a little seaside village called Portpatrick. Charles and Pat's words were so true, the place was beautiful. It is situated on the South-West coast of Scotland only a few miles south of Daily, it has everything a couple of old fogeys desire. Peace, golden sands, plenty of places to eat, Castle ruins, paths along the cliffs, caves and of course spectacular scenery.

During Victorian times it was the main sailing off point for ships sailing to Ireland it being the closest point on Britain to the Emerald Isle. There was a lot of money to be made in those days and guess who was one of the main entrepreneurs.

Yes, you've got it. The Orr Ewing family, they have an estate with an enormous castle like house in the area and have been in possession since the 19th century. They were also responsible for financing the construction of the local golf course, in fact even the hotel we were staying in belonged to them at one time.

Along the shore a bit is a place called Islay Knoll, a lovely area and appropriately a monument sits. It marks the site of the Orr Ewing's family burial ground. Legend has it that the bodies are buried upright to afford them a sea view.

And by the way, another movie which will never be the same to me due to my findings. Colditz, everyone has heard about the castle where Hitler sent the bad boys. Officers who were continually trying to escape, well a Lt Orr Ewing was a POW in Colditz and unsuccessfully attempted to escape four times. He is buried on the Islay Knoll.

The Census year 1851 finds Robert and the family in Bothwell, Ref 625, Enum Book 13, Pge 7.

There was no sign of Anne, Susan or Robert Junior. I found on the Dailly records that Anne had married a John Perrie in 1844 in Dailly.

There is a significant addition to the family one additional son born 1843 named Joseph. Joseph was probably too young to have been a Lanarkshire Coalminer, but my God what an adventurous life this lad had, I'll come to that later.

Although they lived in Bothwell, Robert and his sons would have worked in the coalmines of Blantyre which are less than a mile away. I'll bet this was one of the main reasons he emigrated. These Pits were scrupulously run by literal slave-drivers and were renowned to be more dangerous than any in Scotland. A few years after Robert left there were over 200 miners killed in an explosion and families of the victims were thrown out of their homes into the work-house.

I then found him in the village of Holytown on the 1851 Census, again just a few miles from Blantyre. He vanished for a while after that, no records of births, deaths etc. It was then I came across Phil

Speed who produced a wealth of information which was consistent and had some very interesting facts.

This documentation is available on the address www.thespeeds.com

From Passenger lists available, Roberts's sons Mathew 26, Robert 23 and Samuel 20 all arrived in the US on the 7$^{th}$ June 1852 aboard the Cora Linn from Glasgow. There was also a Jeanette Ewing 25 aboard who was Mathew's wife.

Robert and the rest of the family sailed from Liverpool on the William Rathbone and arrived in the US 15$^{th}$ April 1853.

There is no doubt Robert spent the first 50yrs of his life working and living alongside my ggGrandfather and I am pretty sure they had been very close. I have every respect for Robert he had the courage very late in life to move with a very large family to America, not an easy decision. I'm pretty sure it was heart-breaking for Mathew and Robert to split up.

Anyway, it was probably a case of him like me being fascinated by the 'cowboy's and Indians' ok, ok; I know they did-nae hae the telly or picture hoose's in those days but they would have heard about the wild west through the grapevine. Then again maybe they had no option and were forced to go to America?

As I said I discovered fellow inquisitive Ewing researchers; present day descendants of the Muirkirk Robert Ewing: Phil Speed from Iowa, Jan Weard, Karen Avery, Karen/Dick Childs from Oregon and Tammy Mitchel from Quebec. We collaborated and helped one another enormously.

Robert and his family initially settled in McKeesport, (interestingly a coalmining area),

Pennsylvania, where so many emigrants had gathered.

Then about 1858 they moved to Clayton County Iowa. Quite a distance, probably travelled by rail, the Irish navies having built the rail-road 10yrs previously.

Iowa was the main starting point at this time for the Oregon Trail, it looks like Robert decided not to have a go over this treacherous wagon-train route, of course he would have been 60yrs old at that time. Iowa is where Buffalo Bill, a scout for General Custer was born in 1846.

Roberts sister Nancy had a son called William Lang who had married Mary McDonald in Bothwell, Scotland on the 22nd April 1849. William sailed to Sherbrooke, Quebec around about 1852 and stayed with his mother's sister Anne Ewing Cavanaugh for a time. His next move was on to Ontario where he worked in the Bruce Mines. The families must have made previous arrangements to meet because Williams next and final stop was Iowa.

It is highly likely that William and his uncle Robert worked together at the Holiday Creek Mine in Iowa when William aged 47yrs was tragically killed in an accident.

What adventures did this family have; this was the time of wagon trains being attacked by Red Indians, races across the Plains for staking free land, the great Sioux war of 1876-7, Custer's Last Stand, the gold rush in South Dakota in 1874, Billy the Kid rampaging around the West and of course the infamous blood bath of the American Civil War. With all these cut-throats and murderers about, there is no doubt Robert's family would have had a tale to tell.

Unknown to Robert was the fact that by immigrating to America he had literally 'jumped from the frying pan into the fire'. Regrettably he and his seven sons would have been eligible to fight in one of the bloodiest wars in history, the five-year civil war against the Confederacy. In fact, Roberts youngest son Joseph born in Scotland fought for the Union army throughout the whole five years.

Like his father Joseph deserves a mention; this lad was certainly a hero. A drummer boy in the Civil War on the union side with the ninth infantry Company E. Enlisted Sept.9, 1861, mustered Sept. 24, 1861. Mustered out July 18, 1865 at Louisville with an honourable discharge. He married Lillie Jane Speed on 26 Apr 1870 at the residence of Samuel Ewing (probably his brother) in Clayton Co Iowa. They had 12 children only one son, the marriage ended in divorce in 1902. Lillie remarried in 1903 at the ripe old age of 60yrs and Joseph died in 1905.

What this drummer boy must have experienced; the killing during this war was unbelievable, thousands slaughtered on both sides and he was involved from start to finish. And what about his mother and father; they must have dreaded the proverbial telegram, a nightmare, believe me I've been there. Our own son Alan was a combatant with the 'Royal Scots Dragoon Guard's' throughout the wars in Kuwait and Iraq. That's another story.

When I think of Joseph's experience there is one film which stands out in my mind as being the best for showing true events and representing how parents actually feel when their children are in danger.

Shenandoah starring James Stewart, a Virginian farmer who was not afraid to refuse joining the confederate forces and withstood the anger of his neighbours for taking a stand. When the battles eventually landed on his doorstep everything changed and his daughter in law was murdered by one of Quantrill's men. Well I'm not sure what battles Joseph was involved in but there is nothing surer he became involved with an Ewing General; they were on both sides.

Robert died in Iowa aged 69yrs.
Thankyou. Robert.

# Chapter 27

## American Civil War.

Way back in 1812 a Kentucky Regiment led by a Lt; Col; Young Ewing, a Captain David Ewing, a Lt Thomas Ewing (1789-1871) and a General Ewing decided to declare war on the British and invade Canada.

Thomas Ewing was of Scots/Irish descent and eventually became United States Senator from Ohio (1831-37), Secretary of the Treasury (1841), Secretary of the Interior (1849-50).

Of course, the Americans were chancing their luck; hoping the British resources were totally overwhelmed and incapable of fighting two wars. Battle of Salamanca in Spain where 3x great grandfather Samuel was killed was also in 1812. Well would you believe it; like the cavalry charge to save the wagon train our Lord Eglinton from Ayrshire in Scotland and Ireland with his fiery cross gathered an army and received all sorts of commendations for keeping those American rascals at bay?

They reckon the war ended as a draw? It was said that one of the main reasons the Americans declared war was to stop the British kidnapping American sailors, who were being forced to serve in their warships against the French.

Anyway, when the Americans had had enough of their fighting they got back into the corridors of power. How come so many Ewing's were in these influential positions? Was it because they were well off? Or just because they were educated. They must have been in the know that's for sure and of-course money can buy anything.

Thomas Ewing (1829-96), son of Thomas Ewing, Secretary of the Treasury, at the age of twenty-nine was elected first Chief Justice of the Supreme Court of Ohio. During the Civil War he took a conspicuous part and rose to the rank of General.

The American Civil War 1862. The Confederate's against the Blue belly Unionists. Brother against brother, American against American, what a war. All those emigrants leaving their homeland to escape bloodshed and being caught in this terrible war.

Roberts son Joseph along with many other Ewing's were being asked to kill their fellow kinsmen. Ewing's were abundant on both sides from Generals down to Privates.

Hugh Boyle Ewing, Thomas Ewing and Charles Ewing all Brigadier Generals on the Union side and Colonel Elijah Ewing opposing them as a Confederate. These guys were probably cousins, what the hell were they thinking about.

In September 1864 a Confederate army of 12,000 infantry attempted to seize Fort Davidson a Union garrison of 1,500 men. In charge of the Fort was Brig; General Thomas Ewing, brother-in-law to William T. Sherman. Despite being outnumbered ten-to-one he decided to stand and fight. Brig; Ewing rejected several demands by Confederate's for the Fort's surrender.

This was certainly out of the question knowing there would be no quarter given to himself and his men due to their actions against collaborators of the notorious William C. Quantrill.

After tremendous fighting the Brigadier was given orders to abandon the Fort; he therefore made plans to escape. The Union soldiers stealthily withdrew undetected through the Confederate lines. Having left a slow-burning fuse to their powder magazine the invaders were left with nothing but rubble.

Brig; Gen; Ewing's actions made headlines and eventually received personal thanks from President Lincoln. There is no doubt Joseph was kin to the General as DNA results from many Ewing's in America show close matches.

Believe it or not Ewing's were prominent not only on the battlefield but also in the halls of power in the Whitehouse.

Along with others a Patriarch Thomas Ewing was a confidant of President Lincoln.

Usually history records were only for the well to do, their Lordships being given all the honours and medals, this war changed all that, to a small extent.

A new medal was initiated during this war, only to be awarded to the bravest of the brave. An honour which would be recognised over the years as the highest which anyone could receive and presented by non-other than the President himself.

The Congressional Medal of Honour

America's equivalent to Britain's Victoria Cross. A John C Ewing was a recipient on the second of April 1865. For bravery during the third battle of Petersburg in Virginia. He captured the enemy flag.

John was twenty-three years old when he received this award and no doubt had to fight very hard through waves of sword swinging confederates to achieve his goal.

There is no doubt in my mind this brave lad was a kinsman of mine. OK maybe the connection goes back many generations but according to DNA, there are dozens and more in America who are matches to me.

John Ewing was a Private in Company E, 211st Pennsylvania Volunteer Infantry. You'd better believe it this lad must have done something very dramatic and brave.

I done my best to get further information, no joy I'm afraid. Nothing about his family, no doubt he was kin. John was one of the first to receive this decoration and died on May 23$^{rd}$ 1918.

Chapter 28

## Still in America

I would never have thought for one moment that there would have been anything that could have added to the emotional excitement and entertainment I got from watching 'The Alamo'; When Davy Crocket got skewered and hung up by a Lance on a door and Jim Bowie got bayoneted lying in bed. I was almost in tears.

The movie had it all but there was an emotion missing? One that no film producer could include, one we have all experienced I'm sure. That so strong anxiety and fear for someone very close when their lives are in danger.

Here it was; that extra emotion, I discovered a Ewing was killed at the Alamo. Believe me I have since finding this out watched the film again and again. Sitting on the edge of my seat fantasizing myself in among the slashing sabres and bayonets.

James Ewing fought alongside Davy Crocket and Jim Bowie. He took part in one of the most significant historical and written about battles in the USA and was of Scots-Irish descent.

He was born in Tennessee in 1812, he took part in the siege of Bexar as a member of Capt. William R Carey's artillery company and later served as secretary to Lt. Col. James C Neill, commander of the Texan forces occupying Bexar.

James Ewing died at the battle of the Alamo on March 6, 1836.

Just to give a little insight into what it was like in those days I'll tell a little tale I found very interesting.

A notorious ex-slave bandit and rustler member of the famous "Gault Gang" called 'Isom Dart' (1840-1900) was jailed in a town called Green River. Unfortunate for him he was housed in the same cell as a tough South Pass City miner called Jesse Ewing. Jesse was referred to as the "ugliest man in South Pass City" because of a disfigured face caused by an encounter with a grizzly. Jesse Ewing was reputed to be "mean to the bone" and during the night beat Dart into submission. To add to Dart's humiliation Jesse got him on his hands and knees and act as a breakfast table, Dart was really mean himself and after his release the famous Tom Horn shot and killed him. Of course, Jesse Ewing was not the type to take any nonsense from anyone and would not give up on a grudge. After a dispute with a lad called Coulter Jesse took pot shots at him through a jail cell window. Later he had another go at him even though Coulter was dying on his death bed.

There is no doubt Jesse Ewing was a hard man. This was a hard country full of bandits and gunslingers where men had to be tough to exist. It looks as if Jesse Ewing was also a regular visitor to the Sweetwater County Jail. In 1880 he was held for killing a fellow miner called Charlie Robinson in a gambling dispute. He was found to have acted in self-defence. On another occasion he attacked a Sheriff in Green River. Jesse ended up by getting a wallop on the head with a six-shooter.

Jesse Ewing met his end unfortunately over the affections of a "professional" woman. His adversary a Fred Duncan shot him dead and made off with the Madame.

You know it wasn't only America that got all the excitement, back in 1890, Glasgow in Scotland witnessed on of the most astonishing events ever to hit the city.

Yes, a city where James Ewing owned a very large portion of the land it sits on.

It was on the cobbled road of Duke Street that one of my Wild West heroes Buffalo Bill rode on his white horse. It must have been a tremendous sight. He had with him a troupe of real-life Cowboys and Indians droving a herd of buffalo. What a sight it must have been. Red-Indians with all their feathered regalia and the Cowboys swinging their lasso's and whips. How I would have loved to have seen them.

Buffalo Bill had actually got those Red Indians released from a prison of war camp to take part in his Circus. They had been involved in the Indian wars and had taken part in the annihilation of Custer's $7^{th}$ Cavalry at the Little Bighorn in 1876.

Seemingly the Circus was the biggest show ever to hit Europe. They staged all sorts of acts, Indians chasing Stage-coaches, Cavalry coming to the rescue of fair maidens with the exciting ingredient of arrows and bullets. It must have been a terrific day for all those Glasgow wains (children).

There were plenty of other interesting features to his show. One of particular significance was his sideshow act of the tallest woman in the world. This lady was eight foot four inches in height and that was without high-heels. Somehow, I don't think she would have got many dates, if I had danced with her my nose would have been in her belly button.

She charged 10c for a photograph and 25c for a handshake. I don't think there were any kisses; she was too high and mighty (*boom boom*).

Her name was Ella Kate Ewing 1872-1913 knicknamed "The Missouri Giantess.

With the money she earned a house was built to accommodate her height, complete with an oversize bed. Probably while in Glasgow she slept with her legs and feet sticking out the window.

Paul Newman and Robert Redford, handsome buggers and great actors, their classic was "Butch Cassidy and the Sundance Kid". I loved that Movie especially the "Raindrops keep falling on my head" scene with Paul Newman riding a Pushbike with that beauty Katharine Ross on his lap. Like this Movie Outlaws were usually portrayed as the good guys, mostly untrue but there is one little bit of history which struck me as being just a little in their favour.

I quote:

Albert (Slick) Nard was a horse thief and a member of the gang when he was arrested for the shooting of William Ewing near present day Slick Creek. Nard was sneaked out of Thermopolis by the Deputies in order to avoid him being freed by the other outlaws.

Ed Farlow's statement.
In the morning there was a little excitement when I came over to dress Ewing's wounds. Slick and the deputies were gone and no one knew just how. Several of the boys were at the saloon talking about it. When I rode up, they told me Slick had gone and said, "Yes, I know it. He should be on the top of Ten Sleep Mountain by now on his way to Buffalo". Mike Brown spoke up and asked, "What was the big idea"; I told him straight. "We did not know how soon you fellows would say 'turn him loose.'". Mike replied, "Turn that son of a bitch loose? If you had said the word, we would have helped you

hang him. I want you to know this, Farlow. We may rob a bank, or hold up a stage or a railroad pay car now and then, but we are not killing working men for their money. We are not that damn low yet."

So, what we can take from this is in the territory plagued by outlaws. William Ewing was a working man and respected by the Outlaws. Sounds good to me, these Ewing's are all over the place, and America's full of them. I'll bet like William the majority of them are hard-working honest guys.

# PART FIVE

## Chapter 29

## Salamanca

I'm going to give you the reader a bonus, my 3x great Grandfather Samuel was killed at the Battle of Salamanca, Spain in 1812. As well as explaining Samuels exploits, I am going to tell you about our adventure when travelling to and visiting the battle-site.

Samuel joined the Scottish 74th Regiment that sailed from Cork to join eventually the 3rd Division of Wellingtons army in Portugal in 1810. He was a Lieutenant, meaning his family must have been in a position of some authority and wealth. In those days it was the done-thing to buy a senior position in the army, and by the way a position which allowed his wife to travel with him.

A Lieutenant would have had direct charge over about twenty men and probably members of his own family among them. He would have had certain privileges including being allowed his wife to accompany him, which would explain her disappearance from her son Mathew's life.

The conditions for everyone in the army at this time must have been horrifying, continually on the move in all weathers and having to forage for every bite to eat. As Emilia my 3x great Grandmother was the wife of a Lt; she would have been in charge of the well-being of the troop. Can you imagine it? Twenty exhausted men coming back from a battle some with horrible injuries, hungry and dependant on the help from one or two women. Off-course I mean no disrespect to the women of today but in those days, they were hard as nails cut your leg off no bother individuals.

I believe Samuel had Emilia with him and what an arduous time they must have had on that ship going across to Europe; cramped along with hundreds of soldiers, horses and livestock. All sorts of war material like gunpowder and cannons, they would have been a floating bomb just asking for a French warship to put them to the bottom of the sea. We flew from Edinburgh to Madrid in about three hours. How long it took Samuel to reach Portugal I don't know? certainly more than 3 hours.

My journey to Edinburgh wasn't bad, motorway all the way. the airport was something else though. The busiest airport in Scotland and it lived up to its reputation it was mobbed. If we had not pre-booked our car park we would have been in big trouble, we were parked about a mile away and had to get a bus to the terminal. I shouldn't complain though, I wonder what conditions Samuel and his wife had to endure on their traveling.

Security, they were strict, I almost dropped my trousers when I had to take my belt off. Margaret got a bit of excitement when she got buzzed and had to be body-searched. When we eventually got on the plane, I was sitting beside a giant, very uncomfortable flight. We hadn't even left Scotland and we were exhausted, word of advice; avoid Edinburgh Airport and Spanish airlines.

It was January 1810 when Samuel and Emelia sailed from Cork for the Peninsula, to take their share in the blood thirsty operations going on there, they landed at Lisbon along with the 74th on February 10th. On the 27th they set out to join the army under Wellington, and reached Vizeu on the 6th of March. The Regiment was placed in the 1st brigade of the 3rd division, under Major-General Picton, along with the 45th, the 88th Irish, and part of the 60th Regiment. This division was to perform such a distinguished part in all the Peninsular operations, that it earned the famous title of "The Fighting Division"

Edinburgh airport was bad, Madrid's was ten times worse. The Terminal was like Argyll street the week before Christmas; It was a push and shove move with the crowd queue for the toilet experience. Fortunately, the moving crowd took us to the Exit where the Information Desk was. But unfortunately, they couldn't understand my English with the Scottish accent. We had to find the Bus Station and get to Salamanca and it was getting late, they were anything but helpful, in fact they were totally disrespectful.

The first major action in which the 74th had a chance of taking part and where Samuel was initiated was the battle of Busaco in Portugal on September 27th, 1810 (There had been small skirmishes prior to Busaco). The allied British and Portuguese army numbered 50,000, as opposed to Marshal Massena's 70,000 French-men. The first attack was made at six o'clock in the morning by two columns of the French, both of which were directed against the position held by the 3rd division. One of these columns was thrown back by the fire of Samuel's regiment the 74th. The advance of this French column was preceded by a cloud of snipers, who came up close to the British position, and were picking off men, when two companies of the regiment were brought forward; they drove back the enemy's skirmishers. The French, however, renewed the attack in greater force, and the Portuguese regiment on the left was thrown into confusion, putting the 74th in a most critical position, fortunately the danger was seen and the 9th and 38th regiments were sent to its support. These advanced along the rear of the 74th in double quick time, met the head of the French column as it crowned the ridge, and drove them irresistibly down the precipice. The 74th then advanced with the 9th, and kept up a fire upon the enemy as long as they could be reached. The Allied army lost 1200 men. The enemy lost 5000 killed and wounded.

As I said Madrid Airport was a nightmare, it must have been an hour since we landed. All the cafes were full, couldn't even find a place to sit down and we were getting no-where. The place is enormous it has four terminals and it is a bus journey distance between them, and we weren't sure if we were in the correct terminal to get the bus. We were certainly beginning to panic, I had visions of spending a night in this abominable place.

The 74$^{th}$ moved from Busaco to help in the defence of the lines Tones Vedras, fortifications which were built to defend Lisbon the Portuguese capital. After two months of patrols and repelling the enemy they moved on to the village of Togarro where they remained until March 1811. The Regiment along with Samuel and Emilia suffered much discomfort and hardship from the heavy rains, want of provisions, and bad quarters. On the 12$^{th}$ of March a division of French were found posted in front of the village of Redinha, the Third division attacked and after a short battle the enemy retreated across the Redinha River with the 74$^{th}$ in pursuit. On the 15$^{th}$ of March they were attacking this time at Foz de Arouce where the enemy lost many men. The third division was constantly in advance of the allied forces in pursuit of the French, and often suffered from want of provisions. This situation was caused by the division commander putting his quest for personal glory before the well-being of his men. Disgusting selfishness putting thousands of his men into unnecessary danger.

My 3x great Grandparents were definitely introduced to the horror of the battlefield at Busaco. They now knew what war was all about; and probably realised it was a high possibility with the dangers that lay ahead, they would never see their son again.

Margaret and I have been to Portugal not at the battle site of Busaco but in a resort called Albufiera, in getting there we probably flew over the land Samuel had fought on. A very warm country, the weather can be very unsociable, tropical storms and unbearable heat can be the order of the day. We had a memorable holiday though, paddling through shifting sands on the beach and almost washed off a walkway by a freak wave, another script for Benny Hill.

Here was Samuel with the 74$^{th}$ at the siege of Almeida on the morning of the 3rd of May 1811 where the first and third divisions were concentrated a short distance in rear of Fuentes d'Onor which the 4$^{th}$ division was defending. Several attempts to occupy the village were made by the French who renewed their attack with increased force on the morning of the 5th May. After a hard fight for the possession of the village, the British defenders were nearly driven out by the superior numbers of the enemy, when the 74th were ordered up to assist. The left wing, which advanced first, on approaching the village, narrowly escaped being cut off by a heavy column of the enemy, which was concealed in a lane, and was observed only in time to allow the wing to take cover behind some walls, where it maintained itself till about noon. The right wing then joined the left, and with the 71st, 79th, and other regiments, charged through and drove the enemy from the village, which the latter never afterwards recovered. The 74th on this day lost Ensign Johnston, 1 sergeant, and 4 rank and file, killed; and Captains Shawe, McQueen, and Adjutant White, and 64 rank and file, wounded.

At last we found another Information Desk and guess what one of them understood a little English and seemed pretty helpful. It turned out our Bus Stop was only 100yds away, which was good news but and I mean but, we would not be allowed on the Salamanca bus without a ticket and to get one we would have to go to the other side of the Terminal. We couldn't find the place, went back to the Information desk, they advised us to go back through security where there was a mile-long queue, which to my mind was totally out of the question. After about an hour of exasperation I found an airport security guard and gave her a pleading help me please gesture, luckily, she could speak a little English. She told us that you could buy a ticket on the bus. We still had doubts whether we required a ticket or not. We decided to Hell, even if it meant a bit of bribery and corruption by giving the bus-driver a bung(tip) we would take the chance and get on without a ticket. Even finding the correct bus stance was difficult, our first piece of luck a fellow passenger who was English gave us directions.

You might think I'm going on a bit and jumping back and forward. It's just the way I tell them and in-case you are thinking of travelling to Madrid, think again or take a translator and be prepared.

Thank goodness Samuel didn't have Madrid Airport to contend with. So stupid of me? he had enough problems that's for sure. He was still fighting and marching, in fact he was on the road from Ciudad Rodrigo to Almeida which crossed a ridge near the then recently destroyed fortress of Fort Concepcion. Wellington expected that the French would approach south of the Almeida road, where the ridge levelled off. He placed a strong garrison at this point in front of the village of Fuentes de Oñoro, an insignificant jumble of streets with seemingly strategical importance. Samuel was to experience head to head bayonet stabbing murderous street fighting in this little village along with the First and Third divisions. His Regiment lost many brave men at Fuentes de Onoro.

On 3rd May 1811 the French attacked across the Don Casas and stormed into Fuentes de Oñoro. The fighting see-sawed throughout the day with the French troops forcing their way into the village and being driven out. As night fell the attackers were finally pushed back and the village remained in British hands.

At last the bus came and we humiliatingly were not allowed on the bus, the driver couldn't speak a word of English and swung his arms and hands directing us back. Panic stations again, we hung back watching everyone with tickets filling up the bus, I had visions of us being stranded in this overcrowded hell hole called Madrid Airport.

We were ready to walk away when we saw a couple get on and paying the driver. It turned out that ticket holders got priority so everyone was correct; you needed a ticket; but on the other hand; you didn't need a ticket, luckily there were two seats available and we were on our way to Salamanca. I was bloody exhausted already but too excited to sleep. Our experience had been, to say the least dramatic in fact again, it would have been a wonderful sketch for the Benny Hill show.

Our bus journey from Madrid to Salamanca was reasonably comfortable but almost three hours sitting looking out at barren waste-land can be a bit boring. Any agriculture we seen were a few hay fields being watered by rows of moving sprays. How those soldiers all those years ago managed to survive under these harsh conditions is beyond me. We couldn't sleep, it was too hot. On arrival in Salamanca we passed our hotel the Regio then the Cathedral, the place looked very interesting we'll explore tomorrow. It was now eight pm we had been travelling for fourteen hours. No bother getting a taxi; a bit of sign language and we were on our way from the bus-station to the hotel. He took a roundabout route cost 13 euros for a couple of mile journey. Thank god the hotel receptionist spoke English. After a poor and expensive didn't eat much meal we got the heads down, being totally exhausted slept a ten-hour undisturbed sleep. The first day of our adventure was over and we were still sane?

Samuel had a rest day from fighting on the 4th May 1811, but it seemed the French were preparing to attack. They were at the village of Fuentes de Onoro, Wellington using his intuition marched the 7th Division along with cavalry into a strategic defensive position. On the following day the French cavalry attacked the Seventh Division followed by two divisions of their infantry. There was an immediate crisis, the Seventh Division being unable to hold against such force. Fortunately, due to French mis-haps on other parts of the field they did not press the attack.

Simultaneous with his assault on Poco Velha Massena, the enemy launched a series of overwhelming attacks on the village of Fuentes de Oñoro, which lasted throughout 5th May. The light companies had been replaced overnight by the 74th and 79th Foot, both highland regiments who were supported by the Irish 88th Connaught Rangers.

At the high point of their assault the French drove the two highland regiments to the top of the village. Colonel Wallace counter attacked with his 88th and drove the French out of the village and back across the Don Casas. The French, their ammunition running low, refrained from further action. The 74th Foot lost 4 officers and 66 soldiers at the Battle of Fuentes de Onoro.

The old city of Salamanca is amazing and yet to my mind a bit skin crawling, it is more like the size of a village than a city and is dominated by Church's, Cathedrals and gift shops. There are two Cathedrals and eight churches and of course a Monastery in an area of not much more than one square kilometre. The buildings are enormous, the inside of them are decorated by fantastic sculptures, even the pillars are beautifully carved and designed with cherries and suchlike. Hundreds of old paintings adorn the walls, Jesus on the cross made of marble all over the place. Every piece of wall has decoration or painting. There's a fortune in Gold and precious stones gathering dust behind barriers or in glass cases. The places are overwhelmingly wealthy and yet there are beggars on the street. I'm not a religious person, to be honest I just do not believe and seeing this wealth from all those years ago when people lived in poverty doesn't help matters. Salamanca; sorry; I cannot understand why the British bothered to lose so many men to give you your freedom.

Not only is the Cathedral, impressive, the University has its qualities to and the Plaza which was once the bull-ring is certainly a place to admire and get a cup of coffee. The Romans were here long before the Cathedral, the evidence; there's a Roman bridge over the river Tormes. Anyone who is religious would love Salamanca, I'm not; but was certainly impressed by the size of the buildings, built all those years ago and still standing today. Ridiculous to think; all they had was rope and tackle; our builders have all the mod-coms and can't even construct a school to last a year.

The Salamanca'ns certainly make the most of their popular city, there are walking tours and bus tours all over the place. It is very busy and making big money, especially the Cathedral where they are queuing to get in. One thing that really bugged me; the taxies cost five euro's before they move and they take the longest route, there's a lot of rip-offs that's for sure.

Unexplainable likeness of an astronaut carved on wall of Cathedral which is 900 years old. The intricacy of the carvings is an example of what we seen all over, even on the columns. Truly awesome; the astronaut by the way caused a lot of controversy and drew in the punters until it was disclosed recently that it was done during restoration work in the 1990s… What they will do to make a bob or two.

We were in Salamanca for one reason and that was to visit the site of the Battle of Salamanca. I was under the impression it would have been one of the top tourist attractions; the battle having been one of Britain's greatest victories and the result being Spain's liberation from the grip of Napoleon. What a disappointment; In the Plaza Mayor information centre we were advised not to bother visiting the site, being told the place was long forgotten and there were no tours and no bus's going to the area. Typical; me thinking there would be tour guides and bus tours; stupid of me. A couple of miles away from your precious city there were almost twenty thousand men killed; some gave their lives to free your ancestors from slavery.

The attitude towards the battle by the adviser in the information centre was typical to the feelings of the Spanish people. We visited museums and there was no mention of the peninsular war. Nowhere in Salamanca was there indication that a battle had taken place a few miles from the city. The reason; maybe because the Spanish took no part in the battle, they were positioned to block the French escape route and they made a hash of that. Three thousand one hundred and twenty-nine British, two thousand Portuguese and seven yes only seven Spanish dead. The French lost thirteen thousand men. There is a total of approximately eighteen thousand bodies unaccounted for in the fields just five kilometres south of Salamanca no grave nothing. Shame on Spain and Salamanca; the Allied army of Wellington liberated Salamanca and gave them their freedom from the heel of the French and did not even receive a decent burial. The city and Spain gained their freedom and have shown no respect for the dead, not even recorded the event.

Shame on you Spain. There was a big queue behind us so we gave up in disgust and decided to get down to planning our visit to the site the following day.

The 74th was from the beginning of October mainly stationed at Aides de Ponte, which it left on the 4th of January 1812, to take part in the siege of Rodrigo. The third division reached Zamora on the 7th, five miles from Rodrigo, where it remained during the siege. The work of the siege was laborious and trying, and the 74th had its own share of trench-work. The assault was ordered for the 19th of January.

Immediately after dark, Major-General Piston formed the third division in the first parallel and approaches (Samuel and the 74$^{th}$ again in the forefront), in readiness to open the defences. At the appointed hour the attack commenced on the side of the place next to the bridge, and immediately a heavy discharge of musketry was opened from the trenches, under cover of which 150 sappers, directed by two engineer officers, and Captain Thomson of the 74th Regiment, advanced carrying bags filled with hay, which they threw down the counterscarp into the ditch, and thus reduced its depth from 134 to 8 feet. (Point of interest; I was a sapper in the Royal Engineers, fortunately I didn't see action other than a fight in the Blackpool Tower Ballroom.) They then fixed the ladders, and General McKinnon's brigade, in conjunction with the 5th and 94th Regiments, which arrived at the same moment along the ditch from the right, pushed up the breach, and after a sharp struggle of some minutes with the bayonet, gained the summit. The defenders then concentrated behind the retrenchment, which they obstinately retained, and a second severe struggle commenced. Bags of hay were again thrown into the ditch, and as the counterscarp did not exceed 11 feet in depth, the men readily jumped upon the bags, and without much difficulty carried the little breach. The division, on gaining the summit, immediately began to form with great regularity, in order to advance in a compact body and fall on the rear of the garrison, who were still nobly defending the retrenchment of the great breach. The contest was short but severe; officers and men fell in heaps, killed and wounded, as Cannon blasted them with grape-shot, and many were thrown down the scarp into the main ditch, a depth of 30 feet; The garrison then abandoned the rampart, having first exploded a mine in the ditch of the retrenchment, by which Major-General McKinnon and many of the bravest and most forward perished in the moment of victory. General Vandeleur's brigade of the light division had advanced at the same time to the attack of the lesser breach on the left, which, being without interior defence, was not so obstinately disputed, and the fortress was won.

In his subsequent despatch Wellington mentioned the regiment with particular commendation, especially naming Major Manners and Captain Thomson of the 74th, the former receiving the promotion of Lieutenant-Colonel for his services on this occasion.

During the siege of Rodrigo, the regiment lost 6 rank and file killed, and Captains Langlands and Collins, Lieutenants Tew and Ramadge, and Ensign Atkinson, 2 sergeants, and 24 rank and file, killed.

Another battle which my 3x great Grandfather Samuel had survived and of course our illustrious leaders getting their reward.

Samuel and Emilia would have walked the streets of Salamanca over 200 years ago. Did they visit the Cathedral and all those gold adorned Church's? What a contrast to the poverty they would have left in Ireland. They would have been in the killing fields of the Peninsular for two and a half years, Margaret and I had only experienced the climate for five days and couldn't get home quick enough. We visited the modern part of Salamanca, not very impressive, we booked our tickets for the train back to Madrid, and certainly the railway station is modern and clean. No Charity shops, one large very expensive Marks and Spenser lookalike store, didn't see anything we fancied. Went into a local coffee shop, trouble again no speekee de engleesh. I ended up with a thimble full of coffee, Margaret's we couldn't identify. I'll not go any further into that.

What was it like to be the wife of a soldier during the Peninsular War; Think about it; marching in desolate countryside, not a tree or bush to hide one's embarrassment with thousands of soldiers around to witness their ablutions etc. my 3xgreat Grandmother Emilia would have been a hard lady that's for sure, of course that's a minor detail compared with some of the hardship they endured?

I quote.

A soldier's life in Wellington's day was bleak in respect of domestic comfort. The army actively discouraged the rank and file from marrying; only six men in every hundred were officially allowed married status, with the commanding officers permission – this meant that their wives could live with them in barracks and were allowed to draw soldier's rations. The other camp followers had to shift for themselves, there were no restrictions against such relationships and the soldier's woman could seek work nearby; but their prospects were meagre.

When a battalion was posted overseas the recognised wives were allowed to accompany their men, some even taking young children with them; the strict limits on the number allowed on the ration strength led to heart-breaking scenes as the women were drawn by lots at the port of departure. The 'lucky' women marched with the battalion's baggage, sharing every hardship and many of the dangers of camp life.

On retreats or forced marches their fate was pitiable but it must be said they were often an unmitigated nuisance, blocking roads and accepting no sort of discipline. One cannot fail to be moved however, by their sturdy courage. More than one exhausted redcoat would have been left in the road if his wife had not carried him on her back, musket and all. In the aftermath of battle the wives of titled officers could be seen searching among the piles of dead and wounded for their men. I have certainly given a lot of thought to why my Emilia would have left her infant son Mathew behind and went with her man to the battles in Spain. It is after appreciating from history how important the women were to the soldier that I can understand her decisions. The camp following wives were not only there for the run of the mill day to day caring but also in the aftermath of battle to act as a Florence Nightingale towards the wounded.

The 74th was now sent to take part in the siege of Badajos, which it reached on the 16th of March (1812), The work of preparing for the siege was hard, more-so due to the constant heavy rain. Firstly, there was a French Fort to be attended to, which was battered by cannon and assaulted by 500 men of the third division, among whom were 200 men of the 74$^{th}$. As usual Scots, Irish and Samuel in the fore-front.

The fort was very well defended, seven guns were mounted on the parapets. There were 300 French and every man had two muskets. The 74th advanced about ten o'clock, and immediately alarms were sounded, and fire opened up from all the enemy ramparts. After a fierce conflict, in which the Allies lost many men and officers. The enemy, more than half of the garrison, the commandant, with 86 men, surrendered. The 74th lost many brave men.

On the 6th of April 1812, the assault on Badajos was ordered to take place. The Allies cannons commenced their bombardment. The old walls couldn't take it and soon crumbled giving the attackers a gaping breach. Wellington, in person, gave the order for attack.

The third division including the 74th and Samuel (in the fore-front as usual) advanced against the full force of the French cannon and musket then attempted to scale the castle walls, which were from 18 to 24 feet high.

They spread out and heaved their ladders against the walls, and with incredible courage ascended amidst showers of heavy stones and other missiles. All the while being fired upon and stabbed with bayonets and pikes. The ladders were being pushed from the walls and there were screams and deafening shouts. The 74th were being crushed and had no option but to fall back and take shelter.

A second attack was ordered, additional men brought into the fray. The killing continued until at last an entrance was forced and the soldiers triumphantly established themselves on the ramparts. It is said the 74ths Piper then in full view started playing "The Campbells are Comin" until he was shot through the bag.

After capturing the castle, the third division kept possession, while the fourth and light divisions marched into the town. Their actions according to history being something the British would be forever ashamed off. 4000 non-combatant civilians including women and children were brutally murdered, there was excessive rape and looting. The town was ravaged by drunken brutes who wore the uniform, and in the aftermath, although Wellington had gallows built no-one was reprimanded.

5000 of Wellingtons men died during the siege, including from the 74th, 3 officers and 23 rank and file. There were also 108 wounded. Samuel survived to fight another day.

This was it; against all the odds we were about to finalise our great adventure. After a hearty breakfast it was back to the information centre. I knew exactly what we needed to do and we were determined to do it. My plan was simple, have the adviser write instruction in Spanish for the taxi-driver to drop us at the site of the battle, the village of Arapiles. Then to come back after two hours to take us back to Salamanca, sounded good, the information guy was impressed. I don't know why he didn't suggest this yesterday it would have saved me a restless night. Anyway, his help was free and I appreciated it.

Ten in the morning and it was hot; we got stocked up with water, had a sit for a while with a large cool delicious beer and made our way to the taxi rank.

Two hundred odd years ago it was a different matter, not so hot. The 74th left Badajoz on the 11th of April 1812 making their way to Salamanca and it was very wet. When it rains in this area its tropical, thunder, lightning and bucketing down; we experienced it the day before we left, actually buying brollies for the occasion.

Along with a large portion of the allied army, the 74th was drawn up on the heights of San-Christoval, in front of Salamanca, from the 20th to the 28th of June, where they again at a cost of losing many men captured two forts.

The French then surrendered the town of Salamanca to the British and retreated across the Douro where they were reinforced, the allies then returned to their former ground on the heights of San-Christoval, which they reached on the 21st of July. In the evening the third division and some Portuguese cavalry bivouacked on the right bank of the Tormes, over which the rest of the army had crossed, and was placed in position covering Salamanca, upon one of the two rocky hills called the Arapiles.

This was our destination the village of Arapile and then onto the hilltop of the "Greater Arapile" where we could give our respects to the memorial of the battle. Our taxi driver never stopped talking all the way; we just kept nodding our heads and acknowledging respectfully his Spanish gibberish by replying "gracious". There were very few signs of civilisation on the road just desert and dust. I certainly would not like the prospect of walking it back to Salamanca; God it was warm, 40degrees Centigrade. I hope the driver understands he has to come back for us.

On the morning of the 22nd 1812 the third division crossed the Tormes, and was placed in advance of the extreme right of the position of the allied army. About five o'clock the third division (including the 74th regiment), advanced in four columns, supported by cavalry, to turn the French left, the French was confounded when first they saw the third division, for they had expected to see the allies in full retreat. The British columns advanced in line against musket fire while the French gunners also sent cannon ball and showers of grape-shot into them. The 74$^{th}$ in the front, continued their attack under overwhelming odds, creating havoc amongst the French troops. Even when cavalry charged against them the 74$^{th}$ continued advancing, in fact the French retreated approximately 3miles.

The action by the 74$^{th}$ was regarded by some as one of the most heroic during the whole of the Peninsular war and was applauded by no less than Major General Pakenham.

A quote from a soldier of the day:
Dozens of guns, the shot biting into our ranks flipping men over in crazy somersaults or sending an arm or head on its own jawing into the sky.

Lord Londonderry says, in his Story of the Peninsular War.

"The attack of the third division was not only the most spirited, but the most perfect thing of the kind that modern times have witnessed; Regardless alike of a charge of cavalry and of the murderous fire which the enemy's batteries opened, on went these fearless warriors, horse and foot, without check or pause, until they won the ridge, and then the infantry giving their volley, and the cavalry falling on, sword in hand, the French were pierced, broken, and discomfited. So close indeed was the struggle, in several instances the British colours were seen waving over the heads of the enemy's battalions."

We were dropped off on the outskirts of the little village, a spot recognised by a signpost which stated; "Wellington had had his lunch during the battle". The driver had a good heart, after Margaret giving it a go with sign language, he shuttled us a further half mile closer to the Greater Arapile. We walked a good two miles over pretty rough ground and the climb was a bit arduous, the temperature that day was 42degrees centigrade.

We have travelled over one thousand miles to acknowledge and lay a flower on the base of this small monument? Unfortunately, it has been neglected even adorned by a bit of Spanish graffiti; with lots of rubbish lying around it. Someone remembered and cared; there was a wreath at its base, we spent a little time cleaning up some garbage couldn't get the graffiti off. The place is a very poor remembrance to all those souls who died on this site.

The arduous two or three stops climb up to the summit was worth it with regards to the view which was amazing. You could see for miles in all directions. The hill called the Lesser Arapile in the distance and using your imagination it was not hard to fantasise thousands of men fighting for the supremacy of its higher ground. Wellington used the Lesser Arapile as his viewing point and had his troops along its ridge whereas the French used the Greater Arapile and had cannon firing from there advantageous high ground.

This little statement from someone who was there tells us what it was like.

"Human beings were being torn apart, where there was once a man now lays an unrecognisable piece of flesh and blood. Shot fired from cannon at point blank range into the tightly packed ranks of soldiers. That shot did not stop when it hit its first target."

The battle of Salamanca was not over the Frenchie's still had fight left in them.

Lord Wellington, was munching on a chicken leg while he watched the French manoeuvres through his glass, when he observed the French line extended and straggling along a full four miles across his army's front.

"By God that will do" he is said to have exclaimed, throwing the remaining bit of chicken over his shoulder and leaping onto his horse. (Famous chicken bone story)

After which he rode hell for leather over to the north-east to give his orders directly to his brother-in-law, Edward Pakenham, who was in command of the 3rd Division: "Do you see those Frenchie's on the hill? Get your Division into line, take those heights in your front–and drive everything before you."

The next hour's events proved fatal for the French. (The 74$^{th}$ were part of the 3$^{rd}$ division).

As one British soldier later recorded,

"We were going up an ascent on whose crest masses of the enemy were stationed. Their fire seemed capable of sweeping all before it; we retired before this overwhelming fire, but; General Pakenham approached and very good naturedly said, 'Reform', and Advance There they are my lads; just let them feel the temper of your bayonets'. We advanced; everyone making his mind up for mischief the bugles along the line sounded the charge. Forward we rushed and awful was the retribution we exacted for our former repulse."

(At approximately the same time as Wellington was giving his orders to Ned Pakenham, cannon-shot from the Lesser Arapil tore into the Greater Arapil and the side of our French Marshal Marmont, destroying two ribs and an arm.)

Pakenham drove his men forward into General Thomieres French-men who'd been completely taken by surprise. They managed to get off no more than one round before the feared rolling musketry of the 74th, 88th and 45$^{th}$ was opened up on them.

Pakenham's men crushed the French infantry, the survivors throwing down their arms and running away. Their first job done, they moved on toward the centre of the French line, which was also having more trouble than they'd anticipated–due to those reserves Wellington had and had ordered forward– General Leith's Fifth Division and the cavalry brigade under the command of General Le Marchant.

The battle continued for some time, with the British troops inflicting heavy casualties, breaking the entire French left, taking 2500 prisoners, 12 guns and 2 eagles. A late effort by General Clausel and Bonnet to break the British centre was doomed.

Three French infantry divisions were available to cover the retreat into the wood south of the Arapil Grande and they fought bravely as the whole Allied army pushed forward, driving all before them.

Victory belonged to the Allies!

The Battle of Salamanca or Los-Arapils as it's known in Spanish is known as Wellington's masterpiece. Some French writers have since observed that at Salamanca, Wellington beat 40,000 men in 40 minutes. Which sounds a bit exaggerated; all those men killed in that short time; I don't think so.

The Anglo-Portuguese army fought hard; there were some 14,000 French dead and wounded, with another 10,000 stragglers. Generals Ferey, Thomieres and Berthelot were killed, and Marshal Marmont as well as Generals Clausel and Bonnet wounded. In addition to this, the Allies took 20 guns, 2 Imperial eagles, and 6 colours.

Wellington himself had spent the entire battle galloping among the troops as bullets and cannonball whizzed by him–one bullet striking his saddle holster and bruising his thigh.

For Wellington, the way was now clear to Madrid…and the final push to dislodge the French from Spain and Portugal was now on.

The Allied Army lost approximately 5000 men my 3x great Grandfather Samuel and probably his wife among them. A total of 19000 men slaughtered in those few hours; absolutely staggering.

The Irish and Scots for some reason were always on the front-line in the battles Samuel being Irish in a Scottish Regiment probably putting him in even more danger. I suppose his Lordship regarded them inferior giving them plenty praise but regarding them as cannon fodder. The casualties in the 74$^{th}$ Regiment at the battle of Salamanca were — Killed: 3 rank and file. Wounded, 2 officers, Brevet-Major Thomson and Lieutenant Ewing, both severely; *2* sergeants, and 42 rank and file.

Although a great victory, the French were anything but defeated they fought in many more battles. Two years after Salamanca also on the Peninsular a Lt Daniel Ewing of the 74$^{th}$ was killed at Orthes. A Captain Patrick Ewing of the 94$^{th}$ Regiment also fought at Orthes.

There were certainly a lot of Ewing's involved in the battles against Napoleon. It has to be remembered that only Officers were named on casualty lists. My ancestor lies on the field of Salamanca; I feel I have shown my respect and carried out this visit on behalf of all his descendants.

There are many stories and films referring to the Peninsular Wars and again since discovering Samuel was involved and killed at Salamanca the battles have had much greater significance. One very highly rated author comes to mind Bernard Cornwell; his Sharpe adventures although leaving a lot to the imagination; cover every battle including Salamanca and interestingly Sharpe like Samuel was an Irishman in charge of an Irish troop.

The 74th received many honours throughout the Peninsular war, the major one being the capture of the Jingling Johnny at the Battle of Salamanca, which became the treasured regimental mascot and accompanied them all over the world.

The Jingling Johnny, is a musical instrument, consisting of a pole ornamented with a canopy, a crescent and hung with silver bells, metal jingling objects and an eagle on top. It was a powerful rallying symbol as were colours for British Regiments and a replica is still carried today by the musicians of the French Foreign Legion.

The 74th regiment captured not only Jingling Johnny; they also obtained the French 101sts colonel and its Eagle the gilded symbol the emperor Napoleon had urged them to defend to the death. The last Frenchman to hold the eagle of the French 45th Line regiment had his skull cloven in two from top to bottom by Sergeant Charles Ewart of the Scots Greys, and here it was, having witnessed the greatest battle ever fought. That eagle had been touched by the hand of Napoleon himself – the greatest military commander ever to grace the planet.

The Royal Scots Greys trace themselves back to 1678 when 3 Troops of mounted dragoons were raised in Northern Britain. The Regiment soon became known for its grey horses and the name stuck. Today the "Royal Scots Dragoon Guards Regiment" (the Royal Scots Greys amalgamated with the RSDGs in 1971) wear the grey beret and have the eagle badge as a tribute to "those terrible men on grey horses", as described by Napoleon Bonaparte.

The Battle at Salamanca was looked on by many historians as the turning point of the whole war, Wellington's victory demoralised the French who had previously thought themselves indestructible. Leading up to the battle Wellington's army had been on the march for months, amazingly at times even alongside their enemies the French. Both jockeying for position waiting for a mistake, knowing just one little error could mean disaster. Luckily Wellington won the day.

I often wonder; How did Samuel receive his fatal injury, was it on that initial charge, was he involved in the capture of the Eagle. Was it quick by being slashed by a razor-sharp sabre, maimed by a musket ball or mercifully blown to pieces by cannon? Did he die by being seriously wounded on the battlefield and pitifully having his throat cut by his women-folk; I hope he got it quick and Emilia his wife did not have to put him out of his suffering. Were their wife's witness to the aftermath of the battle, all those bodies lying, in the field, mutilated bleeding to death screaming for assistance, the horrors must have imaged a scene from Hell itself. There were very few if any medics, doctors or nurses to call upon, no drugs to relieve the torturing pain; only loyal wives who would scour the battle-field looking for their men. There is no doubt Samuel my ggg Grandfather lost his life on the battlefield of

Salamanca, I can only imagine how he died; a tear comes to my eye thinking about it.

Far distant, far distant, lies Scotia the brave,
No tomb or memorial shall hallow his grave,
His bones they lie scattered on the rude soil of Spain,
For poor Samuel Ewing in battle was slain.

The.

London Gazette.

*Sunday August 16.*

*War Department-Downing Street.*

*Names of Officers Killed, wounded, and missing.*

*Under the command of the Earl General Wellington.*

*In the Battle near Salamanca on the 22nd July 1812.*

*74th Foot.*

*Capt; and Brevet Major Tompson and Liet; Ewing*

Isn't it abominable that there are no public monuments other than the pitiful graffitied one we seen to the thousands who died at the Battle of Salamanca, in fact there are none for the whole of the Peninsular war?

The soldiers of the Peninsular War are as much deserving of our respect as any other group of British servicemen. The hardships they endured are comparable with any other, in fact more-so, the fact that they had to live off the land, had no medical assistance throughout the campaign and the climatic conditions which they operated under were extreme says it all.

There are no memorials in Spain where the British are mentioned, my experience personally where I discussed the battle in the information centre of Salamanca was typical. They told me there was no interest and the general public know nothing about the battle. I travelled to Salamanca expecting to find a war cemetery, there was none, seemingly somewhere there is a mass grave where the bodies and the ashes of the ones burned were dumped.

My ggg Grandparents arrived in Salamanca in 1812 and their visit was certainly more momentous than ours 202 years later in 2014. We were on the site where Samuel lost his life; we had at last carried out what I had promised myself to do for years. We had respected the demise of not only my ggg Grandfather but also the many brave men who died that horrendous day July 25$^{th}$ 1812.

Thousands died within a stone throw of this little village, if you believe in ghosts and that sort of stuff; this place would be number one for a sighting. A Ghost Town; the place gave me the heebie jeebies.

Margaret and I were almost an hour in the village awaiting a late return of our taxi; it was literally a ghost town. We sat on the kerbside for three quarters of an hour, in forty degrees of heat with no shelter and only seen one lonely soul. I was beginning to worry and imagine we were going to be stranded in this desert. To walk back to Salamanca was certainly out of the question, we had no communication link (phones would not work) and I didn't fancy knocking up a local resident who probably couldn't speak English to ask for help.

To be fair there was a little gift shop come museum in the village but it was closed.

We were sitting there like two lost souls, on the spot where Wellington had had his chicken lunch. We had run out of water and really feeling hot when the taxi arrived, straight back to the hotel for a shower and a pint of cool lager.

Margaret and I had a lovely meal in a Restaurant next to the Salamanca Cathedral wall alongside the river Tormes. The menu was in Spanish and I asked what a certain dish was; he replied "MOO" which I understood was beef. Margaret wished chicken and pointed to another meal on the menu; I gave the impersonation of a chicken; flapping my arms giving it the cluck-cluck-cluck. The waiter went into hysterical laughter; we got a freebee bottle of wine along with our delicious meal and made a point of going back again the next two days.

## Chapter 30

## Clan Ewing

Clan Ewing; I am sceptical, I have never been 100% convinced. Was there a Ewing family on the banks of Loch Fyne, did they originate on the banks of Loch Lomond or anywhere else in Scotland?

There were definitely McEwan's, of that there is no doubt, for Ewing's unfortunately I have found no evidence.

My findings point to the Ewing's being well educated, wealthy families who became Barons and Nobility. Everywhere they went they became entrepreneurs, leaders Politicians and wealthy landowners.

Before I go any further let me say; If I am correct, I am certainly not proud of it. History of course hides the fact that the wealthy were cruel manipulators who were selfish murdering fiends and the gangsters of their day.

The majority of Ewing's including myself who have had DNA results are listed as being kinsmen of Sir Archibald Orr Ewing whose heraldry goes back to the 16$^{th}$ Century English Tudor Royalty.

Another serious point is that I discovered my furthest back ancestor James Ewing 1500-1560 is recorded as being born in England. Now that is really of great concern.

In fact, if my theories are correct and my ancestors were Landowners in both Scotland and Ireland after the Highland clearances and the Famines in Ireland. It must mean they were planted by the king of England. Now there's something to think about.

OK James Ewing an English-man came to Scotland during the 16$^{th}$ century, for what reason? Was he part of an invading army? There had been many battles between the nations at that time including the battle of Pinkie where after an overwhelming victory many English settled in southern Scotland. Was he given a position of authority and stationed in Stirling castle? I'm beginning to think this is highly probable and fearing for his life he done a runner from invading Jacobite's or whatever.

Well what do you think of it so far? Are my cousins thinking on stringing me up? This grumpy old so and so has definitely set fire to the heather.

Do not be concerned though, even if our ancestors had no Clan and were a bunch of scoundrels, the majority of the present-day Ewing's I have had the pleasure of meeting are honest to goodness decent people and remember there are other points of view, mines are probably the hardest to believe.

Many years ago, I got in touch with a group through the internet called Clan Ewing of America. As per the title and as far as I know the members at that time were totally American and I being the grumpy old Scotsman that I am decided to join in with their discussions and maybe create a few arguments. What a time we all had, plenty of chit-chat all in good fun.

There was one subject in particular which carried on and on for years, so much so that it eventually got a bit serious and went as far as the Court of Lord Lyon. The argument was whether the group had the right to call itself a Clan.

It all started off jovially and there were plenty of opinions, then the heather was really set on fire, there were to many like me; grumpy Ewing's and unfortunately the argument got a bit beyond a joke, the Klu-Klux-Klan even getting a mention and some members threatening to resign.

Off-course that shut up the membership and I believe the ball rolling for the change of title and the commencement of forming an official Clan Ewing.

Being part of these arguments, which caused the group so much trouble made me feel a little guilty, mainly because in my opinion the committee members could not have been more helpful and sociable towards me. They are a terrific bunch of people.

The result from all this was that the group renamed themselves Ewing Family Association (EFA).

Their next task was really a terrific challenge. they wished to create an official Clan.

Now this is the series stuff, it's not everyone or anyone who can have the official name of Clan put against their group. There are a lot of hurdles to jump before this can happen. There is a Government establishment which deals with heraldry, Clans and whatever and a good case must be put forward before a Clan can be officially inaugurated.

Like most government departments there are a lot of rules and regulations involved and there was a lot of preparatory work to be done.

Myself I had no involvement in these stages, the man who helped the committee enormously and would eventually become the Clans Commander was John Thor Ewing. I have met John Thor on a few occasions and in my opinion, he is more than capable.

As was the routine with the EFA there were no secrets, everyone was kept up to date with the proceedings, there was constant information sent through the internet.

It is certainly a great organisation and I am proud to be part of it, unfortunately I am the only Scottish member and it is sad that the Americans look on their heritage with more gusto than the majority of Scots. Maybe the forming of a Clan will change this, I hope so.

It wasn't long before the group were prepared and the meeting was arranged with the officials of the *"Court of Lord Lyon"* on June 6th 2014.

It was unfortunate that the meeting was to take place at the Beardmore Hotel in Glasgow Scotland, which is part of the Jubilee Hospital. Margaret and I have some disturbing memories here. Anyway, we'll not go into that, we were invited to attend and cordially accepted.

We arrived a few hours prior to the meeting and met my e-mail friends and cousins from the USA; Karen Avery and her husband, Beth Ewing Toscos with her husband, and Jane Ewing Weippert. Through video link we had Wallace Ewing and David Ewing. They were all committee members of the Ewing Family Association.

Also, amongst others on the Ewing side were Gregor Ewing and Thor Ewing with his wife and children.

Meeting Karen, Beth and Jane for the first time was a very pleasing experience; we knew that we were family and kinsmen from DNA tests and we had a great chin-wag. The convention included a delegation from the McEwan's who also wished to apply for an official clan. There was a lot of pomp and ceremony, introductions, a statement from Beth and Thor and it all went very well.

A few weeks later we got word that the Ewing's were officially being allowed a Clan. Thor Ewing immediately got down to business by creating a website, building up a membership and designing an Ewing tartan.

The Ewing's have been very fortunate in having as their chief John Thor Ewing. He is a very competent and well-educated individual.

Take my word for it, you Ewing's interested in family history, Join the "Ewing Family Association" and become a member of the Clan.

I can be contacted through the Clans and the Associations website. I love a chin-wag. I look forward too many confrontations.

It has been one of the experiences of my life discovering so much about the individuals who were responsible for putting me on this wonderful world. It may sound stupid but working on the book has brought me closer to my ancestors, I feel my discoveries have brought them back. Not of course to life but out of the "being forgotten world". As I said in Chapter One, I did not even know my Grandparents Christian names. I'm sure they would have appreciated being remembered and maybe they will thank me when I kick the bucket and meet them?

I'm not one who believes that there is an after-life and that the dead can be contacted. And I'm not a superstitious or religious person, but I have experienced some things which I believe are unexplainable; phenomena which raised the hairs on the back of my neck and got my heart racing.

We all know of Robert Burns; he was a very popular guy in Glasgow he wrote a lot about ghouls and weird happenings. There is a statue of him in George Square. It was unveiled in 1877 in front of 30,000 people and on the base, there are scenes of a coven of witches seen by "Tam O'Shanter" and there is the Devil playing bagpipes terrifying the life out of Tam on his grey mare Meg. The sculpture was made by a G E Ewing and the Plinth by his brother J. A. Ewing.

I will end my story appropriately in the famous Glasgow Cathedral Necropolis Graveyard where there are 50,000 individuals including many Ewing's buried. If there is such a thing as a ghost, then this is the place you will find them. The tales abide, ghouls been seen chasing knights in shining armour and all that sort of nonsense. Just let me say one thing though "You will not see me roaming about there after midnight".

There is an Ewing coat of arms shown on the window of Glasgow Cathedral. The head of armour on it probably signifies that the original holder was a knight. As I have said on many occasions it is on record that an Ewing was the flag bearer for Mary Queen of Scots and the little flag between the two stars on the coat of arms signifies this.

It would certainly be interesting to know what the other symbols mean. The circles are actually sunning with a face. Again, this confirms the status of the Ewing's in Scotland. They were a very influential and wealthy lot with a powerful say in the countries business.

## Epilogue.

I hope you have enjoyed my story. To think? It all started all those years ago when my 10yr old grandson persuaded me to buy a computer. It was my first mistake, I'm a nuts and bolts, hammer and chisel, Commodore 64 sort of person. This contraption had me tearing my hair out, anyway after reading many manuals and lessons from both my Grandsons, I managed to manipulate the bloody thing.

I got right into the web which was my second big mistake I joined a programme called Friends Reunited. Right away I received a message "Hi I believe you are my Uncle Billy" and it all began, David Crawford my Niece's husband got me right into the nitty-gritty by supplying me with copies of birth and death certificates of my family. This was it; I had caught the infection; the bug was in me and there was no cure. I was one of them, a Genealogist.

Of course, my biggest big mistake, my third in fact was getting involved with those over enthusiastic American Ewing's. I could have spent my time watching the telly or playing golf? Dick and Karen Childs; they persuaded me to give a DNA sample which really opened the flood-gates. Then the Clan Ewing of America; included part of my book in their magazine and gave me so much information I had no option but to continue researching.

OK; I'm only kidding, I appreciate everyone who has helped me in my endeavours

What have I got from all my researching? Well I have the great satisfaction of knowing I have achieved something while being in that unwanted territory of the retired. I've kept my old brain working and made many friends and cousins over the years. I have proved and established friendships with individuals whose ancestors were my ancestors.

All those years ago before the Ewing's were scattered all around the world. Right from when the little baby Eagle Wing was rescued from the Eagle and thereafter for hundreds of years, we had a growing group who eventually consolidated into a Clan.

Thank you everyone and no one more so than my enduring wife Margaret.

And last but not least; Keep the Ewing Family Association and the Clan Ewing going. I love you all.

Printed in Great Britain
by Amazon